10-Minute
Clutter Control
Room by Room

10-Minute Clutter Control Room by Room

Hundreds of Easy, Effective Tips for
Every Room in the House

SKYE ALEXANDER

FAIR WINDS
PRESS
GLOUCESTER, MASSACHUSETTS

Text © 2005 Skye Alexander

First published in the USA in 2005 by
Fair Winds Press
33 Commercial Street
Gloucester, MA 01930

08 07 06 05 04   1 2 3 4 5

ISBN 1-59233-145-9

Library of Congress Cataloging-in-Publication Data available

Cover design by Laura Shaw Design
Cover illustration by Elizabeth Cornaro
Book design by Anne Gram
Printed and bound in Canada

In memory of Joel Schneider

Renaissance man, humanitarian, mathematician,
world traveler, creative powerhouse, seeker, and friend.

April 8, 1943 - September 12, 2004

Acknowledgments

No book is truly a solitary effort. This book could never have been written without the help of my friends, family members, and colleagues at Fair Winds Press. Many thanks to all of you who generously shared your favorite tips and techniques for clearing, organizing, and otherwise dealing with clutter, especially Elly Phillips, Delilah Smittle, Holly Schmidt, Lisa Kaplan, Helen Kaplan, Susan Oleksiw, Kate Flora, Margaret Press, and Sue Erickson.

Contents

Introduction: You Can Do It!

Part One: Clutter and You

CHAPTER 1. A Culture of Clutter   19

CHAPTER 2. What Clutter Says About You   39

CHAPTER 3. The Clutter Connection   55

Part Two: How to Take Back Control of Your Home (and Your Life)

CHAPTER 4. Exits and Entrances: Decks, Porches, Halls, Mudrooms, Doors, and More   93

CHAPTER 5. Dirty Little Secrets: Bathrooms   103

CHAPTER 6. Eating It Up: Kitchens   113

Chapter 7. Media Control: Family Rooms   131

Chapter 8. Private, Keep Out: Bedrooms   143

Chapter 9. Battle Stations: Kids' Rooms   153

Chapter 10. Paper Tigers: Home Offices   165

Chapter 11. Hiding Places: Closets   189

Chapter 12. Cobwebs and Cracked Skulls:
Attics and Basements   201

Chapter 13. Everything but the Cars: Garages   211

Chapter 14. Handy Tips for Handymen:
Toolsheds and Workshops   221

Chapter 15. The Grass is Greener: Yards and Gardens   235

Chapter 16. Traveling Light: Travel Tips to Lighten Your Load 249

Recommended Reading   254

About the Author   256

You Can Do It!

"You can't have everything—where would you put it?"
-Steven Wright

Shortly after I began writing this book, I undertook the most effective—and the most drastic—of clutter-control strategies. I prepared to sell the seven-room house I'd lived in for sixteen years and move to another state.

I began pruning my worldly goods down to the essentials—a ruthless exercise that forced me to examine my values and priorities, not only physically but psychologically as well. I gave stuff away to friends. I held a yard sale. I donated boxes and boxes of books, clothing, and housewares to local charities. I threw a lot of old junk away. I stopped buying anything I didn't absolutely need.

A couple of months later, my plans changed and I decided to stay put, at least for the time being. However, my moving plan had given me a chance to really think about how we relate to our possessions and about the process of acquiring stuff. True, our material belongings have practical uses, financial worth, and aesthetic and sentimental value. But we also invest them with emotional connections, and when emotional reasons for owning stuff outweigh or obscure logical ones, we are likely to end up with clutter.

In the ancient Chinese art of placement known as feng shui (pronounced "fung shway"), our homes and workplaces reveal a great deal about us. In a sense, our homes are three-dimensional Rorschach tests. A feng shui master can tell at a glance what areas of our lives are operating smoothly, where our problems lie, and a whole lot more.

As I discussed in my earlier books, 10-Minute Clutter Control and 10-Minute Feng Shui, each section of your home or workplace relates symbolically to a part of your life: relationships, identity, creativity, knowledge, and so on. Clutter in one of these areas of your home suggests you have problems associated with the areas of your life that are linked with that section. (I'll talk more about this in the following chapters.)

The Hidden Cost of Clutter

At what point do we shift from owning our stuff to being owned by our stuff? In researching an article for *Newsweek*, author Peg Tyre found that, "According to a study conducted by a Boston marketing firm, the average American burns 55 minutes a day—roughly twelve weeks a year—looking for things they know they own but can't find."

That's a sobering statistic! The next time you complain about not having enough time to do the things you want to do, think about how much time you may be wasting in this manner. And how much money are you throwing away, buying duplicate items because you can't locate what you need when you need it?

Many of us are trying to get a handle on clutter—you wouldn't be reading this book if you didn't realize the downside of clutter. Home-storage products have become a $4.36 billion industry, and magazines like *Real Simple* show huge circulation gains during a time when many other magazines are closing up shop. We even have TV shows and websites dedicated to controlling clutter.

Obviously, the problem isn't lack of information or awareness. So what's stopping us from taming our clutter and reclaiming our lives? In his book *Clutter's Last Stand*, Don Aslett lists "101 Feeble Excuses for Hanging on to Clutter," which can pretty much be summed up as procrastination. Most of us mean well, and truly intend to get around to dealing with our clutter one of these days, but that day keeps getting pushed further out into the future. Facing up to long-term and large-scale clutter can be overwhelming.

As I mentioned earlier (and will discuss more later), we have to be willing to address the deeper issues associated with accumulating clutter, be willing to change our old habit patterns, and *just do* it. No more excuses. No more procrastinating.

But you don't have to beat yourself up or see clutter control as an onerous task. You don't have to go "cold turkey" and quit buying stuff altogether. You don't have to move. You don't have to live like a Zen monk and deprive yourself of all but the most meager possessions. Clearing your clutter isn't about suffering, it's about making your life easier.

In the following chapters, I've suggested numerous ways to

make clutter clearing more enjoyable—get the whole family involved and make a party of it, for instance. I also recommend starting small and taking it one step at a time—that's the way clutter accumulated, after all, a little at a time.

Because I've tried not to duplicate the tips and techniques I included in my earlier book 10-Minute Clutter Control, you won't find some of the most obvious and fundamental uncluttering remedies here. What you will find is a lot of practical, workable, easy-to-implement advice from experts in the field as well as from friends and colleagues who kindly shared their secrets to successful uncluttering. If we can do it, you can do it too!

Part One

Clutter and You

CHAPTER 1

A Culture of Clutter

Even before we come into this world, most of us already have lots of "stuff," courtesy of well-meaning relatives and friends. Throughout our lives, we continue to accumulate more and more worldly goods, and when we die we pass our material possessions along to our heirs to add to their already burgeoning stash of belongings.

Clearly, we are a cluttered culture. At no time in history have people owned as much stuff as we do today. A few centuries ago, average individuals could only lay claim to a few changes of clothing, a few pieces of furniture, and if they were lucky, a book or two. Our grandparents probably had only a fraction of the possessions many of us harbor today. To earlier generations, the idea of owning a dozen pairs of black heels or twenty white shirts would have seemed ludicrous. Of course, most of the technical equipment we take for granted—computers, CD players, VCRs, DVDs, and all the associated gear—didn't even exist a few decades ago. And according to Robert Grede, author of *Naked Marketing: The Bare Essentials*, more than 10,000 new products are introduced into the marketplace every year.

"Decades of unprecedented prosperity, coupled with relentless advertising and cheaply produced goods from abroad, have created a perfect storm of overconsumption," Peg Tyre explained in a *Newsweek* article.

As a result, we're suffocating under mountains of clutter. My friend Lynda, for example, used to have so much stuff cluttering her bedroom that she couldn't get to the bed and ended up sleeping on the sofa. But although many of us realize we have way too much stuff, we continue acquiring more until we can't even remember what we've got or where we put it. And we need more and more space to stash all that stuff. In 1970, a new single-family home averaged 1,400 square feet. Today it's grown to about 2,300 square feet.

Even then, many of us still don't have enough room for our belongings and have to rent storage containers to hold the overflow. In the last decade, the number of self-storage units in the U. S. has doubled, totaling more than 13 million according to MiniCo Inc., publisher of the *Self-Storage Almanac*.

How did we reach this stage? Why are we cluttering up our lives, our homes, and our environment? How can we free ourselves from obsessive acquisitiveness and reclaim our territory?

The Psychology of Clutter

From the perspective of feng shui, our homes mirror our inner lives, and everything in our homes says something about us on a psychological level. Our belongings have symbolic meanings as well as obvious ones. How we utilize, display, and care for our property reveals how we feel about ourselves and our lives. (In Chapter 2, we'll look more deeply into the hidden meanings of clutter and what your home says about you.)

Clutter doesn't just "happen," it develops over time. Some people are habitual clutterers, whose homes and workplaces are never orderly. Others are temporary or occasional clutterers, who let things get out of hand periodically due to work or personal time crunches. Once clutter gains a foothold in your home, it tends to spread like kudzu, rapidly taking over your living space until, pretty soon, the process of eliminating it seems overwhelming.

From a psychological perspective, you could compare clutter to crabgrass. Its emotional roots are extensive, entangled, and deeply entrenched, so that sorting them out isn't an easy job. Often we aren't even aware of the emotional associations we attach to our stuff. Unless we understand where clutter begins, however, we probably won't be able to manage it long-term and break its stranglehold on our living and work environments. Let's look at common causes of clutter.

Advertising

In a consumer society, businesses must constantly expand the markets for their products. Advertising is one way of doing this. Companies spend billions of dollars annually to advertise their wares on TV, in print, and through other venues.

Of course, the goal of advertising is to get us to buy stuff, especially stuff we don't absolutely need. Effective advertising encourages us to subconsciously identify with a particular product, so that we believe we will become more attractive, lovable, admired, or powerful if we own it. Automobile ads target our desire for freedom or respect. Ads for personal-care products play on our insecurities about our bodies. Beverage ads suggest we'll be more popular and have more fun if we drink a certain brand. Ads featuring celebrities tap our longing for status.

The omnipresent influence of advertising obviously works—just look around your own home and note how many things you've bought because you saw them promoted on TV or in print. Now ask yourself: How much of this stuff do you really need? Would you have purchased it if you hadn't been impacted by advertising?

Fear of Shortages

Many people who lived through the Great Depression often hoard stuff because they fear the poverty and shortages they experienced in their youth. I once visited an elderly woman who had furniture piled to the ceiling. Her apartment resembled a furniture warehouse more than a home. She reasoned that if she ever fell on hard times again, she'd have plenty to sell.

From the perspective of feng shui, however, holding on to old stuff symbolizes holding on to the past, and doing so can prevent you from moving ahead with your life.

Some people worry that their buying power may diminish in the future, especially after they retire. As a hedge against inflation or anticipated crises, they stock up now on things they fear they might not be able to buy later on. My mother, for instance, used to stockpile food so she'd be ready in the event of a nuclear disaster.

As many spiritual teachers such as best-selling author Wayne Dyer point out, this sort of "poverty consciousness" has far-reaching implications, beyond just cluttering up our homes. Worrying about shortages, poverty, and hard times establishes a psychology of loss that can actually attract the very problems these people fear.

Fear of Change

For many people, change is not only unsettling, it's downright scary. Maybe we wish we could return to a time when life was happier or less complicated. We attempt to hold on to the past because it gives us a sense of stability and identity—and one of the ways we do this is by holding on to possessions that remind us of bygone days. When my friend Susan's mother died, for example, Susan found fifty ball gowns her socialite mom had worn when she was a beautiful and popular young woman, all carefully stored as a testament to her past.

Parents often hang on to their children's toys or clothing long after the child has outgrown them. In some cases, these parents may subconsciously be trying to cling to a stage in their children's development—or their own—during which they felt more content or comfortable. But their fear of letting their kids grow up may be hampering their children's progress as well as their own.

Souvenirs are yet another example of how we connect emotions with stuff. My friend Mary Lou, for example, has two identical Hudson Bay blankets—each purchased during a trip to Canada. Although she admits she doesn't really need both, she is reluctant to part with either because they remind her of two pleasant vacations.

I've met men who held onto ticket stubs from sporting events that took place before World War II, and octogenarians who still kept dried flower corsages from their cotillions. When my father died at the age of sixty-eight, I found his grammar school report cards carefully stored in his office file cabinet. A sixty-something woman I know has an entire room in her home devoted to housing her dolls. Another woman saved trunks full of letters dating back to the 1920s.

It's hard to put a value on something to which we feel a sentimental attachment. I still treasure a teddy bear I was given when I was four years old, for instance, and have no intention of parting with it. While it's natural to want to retain some markers of the milestones on life's journey, holding on to excessive amounts of old memorabilia suggests a tendency to live in the perceived safety of the past, instead of moving forward into an unknown future.

Fear of Letting Go

Family heirlooms are frequently among our most cherished possessions, regardless of their material worth. When we lose our loved ones, we may hold on to their possessions for a while, at least until we can put some distance between ourselves and our grief. But if we can't part with the majority of our loved ones' belongings even long after their deaths, it may mean we're afraid to accept the natural cycle of life and death. Sometimes guilt enters into the picture, too. Perhaps we feel it's disrespectful to get rid of the deceased person's possessions. In such instances, we've confused the stuff with the people who once owned it.

No one is suggesting that we divest ourselves of all our beloved mementos of Dad or Grandma or Uncle Harry. But when the past starts crowding out the present, it may be time to set priorities. A friend of mine, for example, has been renting temperature-controlled storage space for more than three years to hold her deceased father's belongings. Another, who lives in a small apartment, has her grown children storing the stuff her mother left behind more than two decades ago.

When deciding what to keep and what to let go, here are some points to consider.

- How much time, energy, space, and money are you devoting to old stuff?
- What do these possessions contribute to your life now?
- How often do you utilize, enjoy, or interact with these objects?
- What would happen if you no longer had them?

Sense of Lack

For some people, buying stuff can become a way of filling the gaps that exist in other parts of their lives. My friend Nancy, for example, often went shopping when she felt unloved or unappreciated by her husband. Buying stuff served as a temporary, albeit inadequate, substitute for the void she experienced in her unhappy marriage.

What used to be called "keeping up with the Joneses" is another form of letting material possessions pinch-hit for self-worth. People who lack self-esteem may attempt to enhance their fragile sense of identity by purchasing the "right" car, watch, sunglasses, or sneakers.

Others see shopping as a form of recreation. "We live in a society of material affluence that puts emphasis on more...and sees shopping as entertainment," writes James Ennis, a sociology professor at Tufts University in Boston. Instead of reading, gardening, playing bridge, or going dancing as earlier generations might have done, many of us shop when we want to amuse ourselves or socialize. Kids in the 1950s gathered at the local park or playground, whereas today's young people hang out at the mall.

Giving ourselves a treat now and again or celebrating an important moment with a well-deserved splurge may be good for the soul. But we set ourselves up for clutter problems (and perhaps financial ones as well) if we buy stuff as a way of compensating for everyday disappointments, insecurity, boredom, or anxiety.

Possession Obsession

Pop artist Andy Warhol had a passion for stuff. Whenever he found something he liked, which happened frequently, he bought it—and stored it. His possession obsession took up hours a day, nearly every day, during which he scoured Manhattan's upscale galleries and flea markets for everything from Mexican ceremonial masks to Fiesta ware. He accumulated so much stuff that Sotheby's netted $25,313,238 auctioning off part of his collection in 1988.

Art patron Isabella Stewart Gardner traveled the world for thirty-five years, gathering all sorts of oddities and treasures. Her international shopping expeditions yielded more than 2,500 paintings, sculptures, pieces of furniture, tapestries, rare books, and architectural remnants spanning thirty centuries, which she shipped back to her eclectic Boston mansion (now a museum).

Collectors are notorious for "over-buying." Imelda Marcos, for example, is probably better known for her 3,000 pairs of shoes than for her political career. Whether the quarry is stamps, toy trains, or first-edition books, the collector's goal is usually to amass as much as possible of whatever it is he or she fancies. The hunt itself becomes a quest-like challenge and the collector's appetite is never sated. Like the adventurer who is always looking toward the next horizon, the collector is always in pursuit of the next acquisition. The thrill of the chase can become addicting, making decluttering especially difficult for these people.

Recently, I attended a convention of beach-glass collectors. Some of these people had spent decades meticulously combing America's coastlines and had gathered more than 30,000 shards of sea- and sand-scrubbed glass. Despite the fact that bits of broken glass now occupied hundreds of jars and boxes stashed in their homes, they continued to go out hunting for more and weren't interested in selling the pieces they already owned.

A funny story is sometimes told about publishing tycoon William Randolph Hearst. An inveterate and disorganized collector, Hearst was busily buying up as much artwork as he could for his castle at San Simeon, California, when he spotted a painting in a catalog that he could not do without. He dispersed agents to search the world until they found the painting. Eventually they did—in one of Hearst's many warehouses. He already owned it.

Confronting Your Clutter

Obviously, there's more to clutter than meets the eye. Do you recognize yourself in any of the previous scenarios? If so, confronting clutter in your home may prompt you to reassess certain attitudes or patterns in your life.

Getting rid of clutter will undoubtedly have an impact on your emotions as well as your environment. Therefore, you may want to take it slow, clearing out one area—or part of an area—to see how it affects you, rather than doing a wholesale sweep. In Chapter 2, I discuss various clutter-clearing strategies you may wish to try, since what works for one person might not be comfortable for another.

When I'm trying to decide what to do with a piece of clutter, I ask myself two questions: Will I use this? Do I enjoy it? This help me bring the object into sharper focus. It's a useful trick when you are trying to decide what stays and what goes.

Unless we deal with the root causes of clutter and the psychological dynamics that led to clutter-mania in the first place, however, we're not going to conquer the problem. As Peg Tyre points out in *Newsweek*, "A one-time cleanup won't solve the problem—any more than a crash diet will cure lifelong bad eating habits."

10 Things to do Right Now

However, if you're eager to get started right away, here are ten things you can do right now that will give you a real sense of accomplishment. Once you see how good you feel after getting your feet wet with these clutter-clearing tips, you may find you can't wait to try the hundreds suggested in Chapters 3 through 16.

1. Get rid of the biggest stuff first.

You'll see immediate results if you attack a cluttered area and eliminate the biggest pieces first—the exercise bike no one rides or the giant panda you won four years ago at the county fair. Making a noticeable dent in your clutter can help motivate you to continue with your task.

2. Return borrowed stuff.

One of the easiest and least painful ways to reduce clutter is to return all the stuff lying around your home that belongs to someone else. Books and magazines are probably the biggest offenders, but other people's housewares, CDs, videos, clothes, toys, appliances, and tools can add to your own clutter. Make a point of returning things you've borrowed as soon as you finish using them—friends are more likely to lend them to you again, too, if you don't abuse the privilege.

> **TIP:** It's easy to forget whose book or CD is whose. Put a return-address sticker on anything you loan, so it can be identified as yours.

3. Pick stuff up off the floor.

If you don't have time to do a thorough pick-up right away, at least collect the stuff that's scattered on the floor. Stash everything in a laundry basket, large box, or trash bag until you can deal with it properly. Your home will look neater instantly.

4. Gather up newspapers, magazines, and catalogs.

Newspapers, magazines, and other reading materials scattered about can really make your home look messy. Recycle or toss those you've finished reading and shelve the rest. If you don't have time to sort through them immediately, at least collect them in a basket or box until you can organize them properly.

5. Go through your closet and get rid of ten things you haven't worn lately.

Most people wear 20 percent of their clothing 80 percent of the time. How much of what's hanging in your closet is just taking up space? Collect ten garments you haven't worn in the past year and take them to a consignment shop or donate them to charity.

6. Wash the windows.

Clean windows let the sunshine in to light up your interior, literally and figuratively. When the windows are clean, everything looks brighter and more cheerful, instantly.

7. Empty wastebaskets.

Trash represents the past—old, outdated, useless things we no longer need or want in our lives. Empty all the wastebaskets in your home as a way of demonstrating your willingness to change old patterns and clear your environment of old stuff.

8. Remove odd socks from your drawers.

Socks that have been separated from their mates for more than a couple of weeks are probably destined to remain solo. Remove them from your drawers and turn them into dust cloths.

9. Clear your desktop.

The fifteen square feet of space on your desktop is precious. Go through paperwork that has accumulated on your desk and act on it, file it, or toss it. A cluttered desk can make you feel overwhelmed by the tasks before you. A clean desk invites you to jump in and start new projects.

10. Throw out pens that don't work.

How many times have you grabbed a pen to jot down a message, only to find it's out of ink or clogged? Don't let useless pens annoy you again—throw them away *now*.

CHAPTER 2

What Clutter Says About You

Believe it or not, your clutter can reveal a lot about you—at least, according to the ancient art of placement known as feng shui. Symbolism plays a large part in feng shui. According to feng shui's tenets, everything in our homes corresponds to something in our personal or professional lives. That's why a feng shui master can quickly size up your financial, romantic, and psychological conditions simply by glancing at your living space. (In my books

10-Minute Feng Shui and *10-Minute Clutter Control*, I discuss this concept in more depth.)

Clutter usually symbolizes confusion, lack of focus, chaos, instability, or muddled circumstances. When we use the word "clutter" we mean an accumulation of too much stuff, without proper organization or distinction. If your home is cluttered, it could be a signal that you have too much going on in your life and your busyness is generating confusion. You may lack direction or priorities. Perhaps you are scattering your energy, rather than dedicating yourself to what's really important. The messiness in your living or working space indicates messiness in other areas of your life.

In some instances, clutter can suggest that you aren't certain about your goals, your identity, your purpose, or what you want from life. Kids' rooms are often cluttered because they haven't sorted out these personal matters yet. In fact, ordering their belongings and organizing their rooms can help children handle important issues in their lives. Studies show that young people who keep their rooms tidy tend to do better in school and are generally better adjusted.

As I mentioned in the previous chapter, clutter—especially old stuff that's been gathering dust for some time—often represents old psychological stuff you are still holding onto. Physical baggage equates with emotional baggage. To a feng shui practitioner, the cluttered areas of your home relate to areas of your life that are stuck or problematic.

Here's a story to illustrate what I mean. Recently I decided to sell a house I'd lived in for sixteen years. For me, the process was quite unsettling, partly because I'd moved around a lot during my childhood and having my own house all these years represented security to me. One of the rather onerous chores I had to undertake before I put the house on the market was cleaning out the basement. In feng shui, the basement represents your subconscious, your past, and your foundations. As I began tossing the old junk that had accumulated down there over the years, I started feeling less stressed out about moving. The physical act of clearing clutter from my basement helped clear up some of my old security issues.

If you've got lots of old stuff cluttering up your home, you may be creating obstacles for yourself and limiting your happiness, prosperity, and personal growth. Once you clear out some of the clutter, you'll unclog areas in your life that have grown stagnant and make room for new people, opportunities, and experiences to come your way.

Different Kinds of Clutter
(and What Each Reveals About You)

Clutter comes in several "flavors," and each represents something different. As you assess your own home, you may begin to see yourself in one of these clutter "types." Over time, your clutter patterns will probably change as your life circumstances change. Here are some of the most common types of clutter and what they reveal about you.

• **New clutter:** This usually indicates that you are trying to do too much, that you lack focus and direction, or that you are letting things distract you from your primary path or purpose. New clutter can include piles of CDs, clothing lying around, toys or sporting equipment scattered about—things you've used recently, but haven't bothered to put away. Our fast-paced, multi-tasking lifestyles tend to produce this type of clutter, and most of us have it to some degree. Clearing and organizing new clutter can help you become more centered, purposeful, and effective.

• **Old clutter:** This refers to outdated stuff you haven't used in ages and might have stashed in the basement, attic, closets, or garage. Old paperwork in your files and old documents in your computer fall into this category, too. Lots of old clutter suggests you fear letting go of things that no longer have purpose in your life, even though they may actually be holding you back. Perhaps you are living in the past, are letting old ideas or emotions govern your present behavior, or are too security-conscious. A good example is my friend Susan's mother, who died in 2002 and left behind files full of old newspaper clippings dating back to the 1930s when she was a young woman.

• **Disarray:** Disarray and disorganization in your home suggest confusion. If you're like most people, some areas of your life are messy or unsettled. The amount of clutter, where it tends to collect, and how long it's been there will show what parts are disorderly and whether this is a temporary or chronic situation.

• **Old baggage:** Old, outdated items you no longer need or use suggest you are holding on to old ideas, attitudes, grudges, fears, or habits. These old issues clutter your psyche and prevent new opportunities from entering your life. The more clutter you have of this type, the more substantial the problem is. Where you dump the clutter reveals which areas of your life are stuck.

• **Large-scale clutter:** Piles of clutter represent obstacles that are limiting your progress. Physically, they hamper your movement; psychologically, they indicate that you are blocking your own growth and possibilities. The more clutter you have, the more you tend to hobble yourself. By cleaning up the physical clutter around you, you can actually sweep away obstacles in your life—sometimes overnight!

• **Broken or damaged stuff:** Broken or damaged objects symbolize disappointments in life: broken promises, shattered dreams, unfulfilled hopes. The areas where the non-functioning items are located will show the parts of your life in which you've experienced disappointments. Damaged furniture, appliances, or systems in the central portion of your home can signify health problems. A faded bedspread could indicate that your love life has grown dull.

The Rooms of Your Home and What They Say About You

Like most philosophies, feng shui encompasses many schools of thought and each path approaches the subject somewhat differently. In my earlier books, *10-Minute Feng Shui* and *10-Minute Clutter Control*, I explain this in more detail and show you how to analyze your home using a tool called the "bagua" from the Black Hat School, which is probably the most popular type of feng shui in the West.

For our purposes here, though, I'd like to offer a less complicated yet effective method for understanding and uncluttering your living space. This simplified system links each room of your home with an area of your life, according to the room's primary purpose.

As I mentioned earlier, much of feng shui is based on symbolism. For example, the family or living room is used for socializing, so it corresponds to your social life, family interactions, friendships, and leisure activities. The bedroom is a place for privacy and intimacy, so it's associated with romantic relationships. The home office, where work is performed, relates to money and career.

Entrance

The entrance to your home is the first thing visitors see. Therefore, it is akin to their first impression of you—the face you show the world, the public image you portray to others. Some feng shui schools of thought emphasize the home's front entrance, but I recommend paying special attention to the entrance you use most often, regardless of whether it's the front, back, or side door.

An attractive, easily accessible entryway presents a positive self-image and makes guests—as well as residents—feel welcome in your home. A cluttered one immediately conveys disorder, confusion, and an unclear sense of self.

Living/Family Room

The living or family room is the part of the home where the occupants tend to come together to socialize. This is also where you entertain guests. Therefore, this room is connected with your social life, friendships, and family relationships. Because this is usually the main room in the home, it also influences your overall happiness and sense of well-being.

A cheerful, comfortable living/family room encourages positive social interactions and rewarding friendships. A cluttered living/family room can lead to confusion, obstacles, or disagreements with companions.

Kitchen

This is where meals are prepared, so the kitchen symbolizes nourishment. From the perspective of feng shui, the kitchen is also connected with your prosperity, and its condition reveals a great deal about your financial situation.

A clean, efficient kitchen suggests that you are comfortable with money matters and aren't troubled by financial woes. A disorganized, cluttered, or dirty kitchen indicates confusion, difficulties, or conflicts where money is concerned. And, because nutrition is integrally linked with health, a cluttered or dirty kitchen poses potential health risks as well. As you analyze your kitchen, think about the symbolism it presents—this is what you are "feeding" yourself and your loved ones.

Dining Room

Usually located between the kitchen and the living room, the dining room combines the qualities of these other two rooms. This is where we nourish ourselves and interact socially. From the perspective of feng shui, the dining room's condition provides clues to understanding your social life, your family relationships, and your finances. The dining room also has an effect on your health, because food is consumed and digested here.

Often the dining room is used for just about everything except dining and may end up pinch-hitting as an office, hobby area, or general dumping ground. Consequently, it's not uncommon for clutter to build up here. A cluttered dining room—especially one that is also used for other purposes—can suggest confusion, stress, or discord in the life areas mentioned above. Cleaning up this undervalued room can have a positive impact on many parts of your life.

Master Bedroom

We spend about one-third of our lives in our bedrooms, so it's no surprise that these rooms have a profound influence on us. A bedroom reveals a great deal about the person who sleeps there—particularly regarding his or her private life, as the bedroom is the place where private, intimate activities (sleeping, dressing, making love) occur. Often, a cluttered master bedroom suggests confusion or discord in a relationship. Broken or worn furnishings can signify breaks in communication, unfulfilled dreams, or a relationship that has lost its spark. Clearing clutter can improve problems in a primary partnership or remove obstacles that may be interfering with the start of a new love relationship.

Kids' Rooms

Children's bedrooms reveal their occupants' personalities, concerns, strengths, weaknesses, and pertinent issues. As every parent knows, clutter is pretty much a given in kids' rooms—not because young people are inherently slovenly, but because they are struggling with so many circumstances involving goals, identity, and self-esteem. This uncertainty and disorder on a psychological level tends to materialize physically as clutter. As I mentioned earlier, training kids to keep their bedrooms clean and orderly can enhance focus, organization, and direction in many areas of their lives.

Bathroom

The bathroom—and your home's plumbing system—correspond to your elimination system. It is here that personal cleansing rituals are performed and where wastes are flushed away. A place for purification, the bathroom is also connected with your health.

In an obvious sense, germs can collect in a bathroom that is dirty or in bad repair. Symbolically, a cluttered bathroom suggests that your body's natural ability to flush impurities from your system is impaired or that your health may be adversely affected by holding on to emotional issues, fears, and confusion related to your private body functions.

Home Office/Study

Home offices are becoming increasingly common as more people work out of their homes or bring work home with them. As you might expect, a study or work area in your home relates to your career and finances. From the perspective of feng shui, the condition of this room describes your attitudes toward money, your ability to attract wealth, your career goals, and your overall work situation.

A cluttered, disorganized office suggests confusion, obstacles, or stress in connection with money and/or your job. If your work area is jammed with lots of stuff, you may have trouble attracting new opportunities or money—there's no room for anything more to come into your life. An office that is neat, clean, and orderly, on the other hand, indicates clarity regarding your career goals and finances. Broken or damaged furnishings or equipment can symbolize breaks in communication, deals that fall through, or financial losses. Fix them promptly to avoid further disappointments.

Attic

From the perspective of feng shui, the attic symbolizes the mind and our thinking processes. Although we may stash stuff we don't want to deal with in our attics and keep it out of sight, it's never really out of mind, and the burden of all that clutter can take a toll on us psychologically.

Attic clutter suggests a lack of mental clarity and general confusion that prevents us from effectively handling the important issues of our lives. An attic crammed with old stuff often signifies old attitudes or ideas that are keeping us from embracing the present and moving forward into the future. In some instances, cluttered attics can result in headaches, tension, and other head-oriented complaints. Clearing clutter can result in greater clarity, reduced stress, and an improved perspective.

Basement

As I mentioned earlier, the basement corresponds to the subconscious, the past, and your sense of security. Like attics, basements are one of the primary clutter zones. But even though we may dump our unwanted stuff in the basement and shut the door, the psychological implications remain.

A basement full of old, castoff stuff suggests you are holding on to outdated issues and behaviors. Perhaps you are being governed by obsolete patterns from your past, and this is interfering with you sense of security. Clearing away the old junk can help to free you from emotions, habits, or fears that may be inhibiting your personal growth.

Garage

I know a man whose garage resembles a warehouse—it's so full of stuff he has to park his car in the driveway. Like basements and attics, garages often become catch-alls for clutter. We don't want the stuff in our immediate living spaces, but we aren't quite ready to part with it either, so we shift clutter to a temporary holding zone where it may languish for years.

In Western culture, the car symbolizes freedom and mobility. If your garage—the car's home—is jammed with stuff, you may be stifling your independence and movement. A clean, orderly garage, on the other hand, encourages pleasant trips and an eagerness to expand your horizons.

In Part Two, I offer hundreds of tips and techniques for uncluttering each room of your home. As you apply these tips, keep in mind the symbolism associated with each room. Pay attention to the feelings you experience during the clearing process and the results that follow—they could be quite fascinating.

If you decide to pursue feng shui more seriously, I urge you to explore other methods for assessing your living and work space as well. Each school of thought has its own distinct advantages and disadvantages, perspectives and purposes. Try them yourself and see which one works best for you.

CHAPTER 3

The Clutter Connection

Clearing clutter in your home is like weeding a garden so the flowers have room to thrive—and you can actually see them! If your dining table is littered with newspapers, magazines, and junk mail, you won't be able to enjoy an attractive centerpiece. Piles of clothing draped over a Victorian boudoir chair will completely obscure its graceful lines.

Clutter also makes it harder to keep your home clean—you have to shuffle mounds of stuff around in order to dust, vacuum, or wipe down a countertop. Disorder and dirt continue to build on one another, and the cycle keeps expanding until housekeeping becomes an overwhelming task.

Deciding what to save and what to toss is a personal matter, and each of us will make different choices. In my opinion, the advice of English designer William Morris provides wonderful guidelines for paring down clutter: "Have nothing in your houses that you do not know to be useful or believe to be beautiful." When I measure my possessions with this yardstick, I have no trouble determining whether something stays or goes.

Sometimes even beautiful things may outlive their purpose in your home. Recently I gave my sister a lovely antique clock that had been in our family for three generations—she wanted it, and I'd looked at it every day for a dozen years and felt it was time for a change. I also passed along a set of delicate porcelain cups and saucers I'd enjoyed for decades, because I'd grown tired of carefully washing them by hand.

If you can't make up your mind, box up articles you aren't ready to part with yet. Label the boxes and store them for a period of time, perhaps a year. At a later date, you can reconsider how important they are to you.

Clutter-Clearing Styles

There's no right or wrong way to clear clutter from your home. Some people prefer to dive right into the deep water, so to speak, and start with a heavy-clutter area such as a basement or attic. They blaze through the accumulation as if they were hacking through a jungle with a machete. One of the satisfactions of this "take no prisoners" style is that it allows you to see dramatic results at the end of the day. Other folks are more comfortable wading in slowly—organizing a spice rack or medicine cabinet, for instance—and then gradually working up to the really big jobs.

An approach that works for many people is to start in the room where you spend the most time. Or choose an area that you'd really like to get in shape. You may wish to follow feng shui's symbolic guidelines and begin with the room that relates to the area in your life that's causing you the most trouble.

Focus on one room or one section at a time, rather than doing a little clearing here and a little there—you'll notice greater results. The sense of satisfaction you'll derive from finishing this job will help inspire you to tackle clutter in other parts of your home.

Often it's easier to do a little at a time, every day. If you spend only ten minutes a day picking up clutter, you'll make progress. This "easy does it" approach prevents burnout and helps you establish a regular clutter-clearing routine.

Find your own comfort zone and proceed in whatever manner works for you. The important thing is to keep at it. As you clear away your clutter, remember this Buddhist saying: "A journey of a thousand miles begins with one step."

Managing Your Clutter

Essentially, clutter management can be broken down into two categories: reduction and organization. Each is important; both are necessary. Organizing your clutter will certainly improve your home's appearance and make it easier to find what you want, when you want it. But you also have to make a commitment to getting rid of the unnecessary stuff you already own and limiting the amount of new stuff you bring home.

My mother is a great organizer. During her "apocalyptic phase," as I call it, she stockpiled quantities of food and other essentials under beds and in closets, in the event that the worst-case scenario came to pass. Everything was neatly stacked and ordered, and she attached typed lists inside the closets cataloguing each item's position so she could locate it quickly. But my mother is also a great collector. When she and my stepfather decided to move to their present home, it took them a year and at least five yard sales to sort out and unload the excess!

The best way to manage clutter is to stop it before it starts. Every time you consider acquiring something, ask yourself the following questions:

1. Do I really need/love this?
2. How much will I really use it?
3. What will it contribute to my life?
4. Is there another way I can obtain the benefits of this item without adding it to my present collection of possessions?

For instance, I love books, but question #4 keeps me from purchasing classics that I can easily borrow from the library. I also love clothes, but question #2 prevents me from buying special-occasion garments unless I have a special occasion that demands it and I don't already own something that's suitable.

However, I do allow myself to acquire one thing each year that I truly love and that I feel will contribute something meaningful to my life. Usually it's something with aesthetic rather than practical appeal—a painting, an antique ivory statue of Kwan Yin, or a mink teddy bear. But I must be able to give positive answers to questions #1 and #3 before I let it into my home.

Clutter-Clearing Strategies for Your Entire Home

In Part Two you'll find hundreds of clutter-clearing tips for every room in your home. Right now, though, I want to share my favorite general methods for eliminating clutter throughout your home and/or workplace. There are plenty to choose from! Use the ones that appeal to you on a regular basis to keep clutter at bay.

Clutter clearing doesn't have to be an intimidating chore. Devise your own personal strategies. Share tips with your friends. Get the whole family involved. Ask everyone to come up with one new way to control clutter. Be creative!

Collect ten things in ten minutes.
Several times a year—maybe quarterly or even monthly—organize a ten-minute clutter-busting brigade in your home. The challenge: Each family member has ten minutes to come up with ten things he or she is willing to part with. If you wish, you can inject an element of humor or competition into the process. Give a prize to the person who comes up with the most useless, peculiar, outdated, or gross object—a thirty-year-old container of Silly Putty, a box of melted crayons, or a malfunctioning umbrella that resembles a dead crow. Give away, recycle, or discard the superfluous stuff.

Start by organizing the things you love.

Sorting, organizing, neatly displaying, or otherwise ordering the objects you treasure—family photos, *objets d'art*, etc.—will give you pleasure. If you start your uncluttering venture with these, the positive experience will inspire you to continue with the task.

Start by organizing things you work with often or enjoy using.

This practice is like the one above, in that it connects uncluttering with something positive. If you enjoy cooking, start by organizing your pots and pans, cooking utensils, and so on. If you have a favorite hobby, begin getting your arts-and-crafts supplies in shape. Once you have a little positive reinforcement under your belt, you can tackle the less savory chores.

Get rid of the biggest stuff first.
You'll see immediate results if you attack a cluttered area and eliminate the biggest pieces first—Great Aunt Laura's battered rocker or that giant dog bed Homer never would use. Making a noticeable dent in your clutter can help motivate you to continue with your task.

Put things away as soon as you finish using them.
Disarray and clutter can't collect if you pick up after yourself—and get everyone else in your household to do the same. As soon as you are through with something—dishes, clothing, magazines, tools—put them back where they belong.

Get rid of things that conjure up bad memories.

Why hold on to something that doesn't make you feel good? Sell, give away, or toss everything that you connect with unpleasant people or situations. As I mentioned earlier, my sister recently said she'd like to have a brass mantel clock similar to the one that had been sitting in my living room for more than a dozen years. The clock had belonged to our grandfather, whom I never liked. I was happy to pass it along to her and get rid of a regular, unhappy reminder of Grandpa.

Do a "walk-through" assessment of your clutter.

Before you begin, go through your home with a notebook and objectively evaluate the situation. Make a list of what you want to tackle first, what can be dealt with later, and what areas you might need to enlist help to handle. After you've gone through your entire home, sit down and prioritize. Set goals and objectives for yourself. This preparation and planning step will help you save time and use your energy efficiently.

Don't clear clutter when you're angry or upset.
Because clearing up clutter can be a disconcerting and stressful task that may trigger emotions you weren't aware of, don't undertake it when you are angry. Choose a time when you feel upbeat and confident. If you sense your mood starting to shift or you feel overloaded, take a break. Or, stop and come back to the job on another day, when you feel better.

Make a date to clean up clutter.
Our lives are so cluttered with activities that you may actually have to pencil in a date and time in your Day-Planner for cleaning up clutter. Schedule a convenient time, preferably once a week, to address clutter problems in your home or workplace. If you set a standing date to do this at the same time each week, you'll soon condition yourself to see clutter-clearing as part of your regular routine—like grocery shopping or getting your nails done.

Hire a babysitter.

Make a date to clear your clutter—and be sure you won't have any distractions or interruptions. Arrange for a babysitter to mind the kids so you can give your full attention to the task at hand.

Turn off the TV.

The TV can distract you from your primary purpose. Turn it off. Let the answering machine take your calls, too. Treat clutter-clearing as you would any other important engagement, and don't allow interruptions to preempt your "date" with clutter.

Have a clutter-clearing party.

Make clutter-clearing an event. Choose a date—quarterly, monthly, or whatever your needs and schedule dictate—and get everyone in the household to participate. Serve refreshments while you work. Play music. Make it fun.

Work when you are at your energy peak.
We all have upswings and downswings in our diurnal cycles. Set a time to clear clutter when your energy level is high. When you grow tired or feel your enthusiasm start to flag, just stop. You can pick up where you left off another day. The point is to feel positive about what you are doing, not to let yourself get overwhelmed or exhausted.

Beat the clock.
Donna Smallin suggests a variation on this clutter-clearing "game" in her book *Organizing Plain & Simple*. She recommends giving each child a basket, pillowcase, bag, or box. Then, set a timer for a period of time—say, ten minutes—and challenge kids to compete to see who can pick up the most useless or unwanted stuff before the bell rings. The winner gets a prize. No, not more "stuff," but maybe a movie or pizza.

Engage the whole family in a clutter-clearing scavenger hunt.

In *Cut the Clutter and Stow the Stuff*, Lori Baird includes a scavenger-hunt checklist for cluttered households. She recommends giving each family member a list of two dozen common, no-longer-usable items, such as odd buttons to unidentified shirts, half-burned birthday candles, dead batteries, and keys to unknown locks. Allow participants a set amount of time to collect these objects. At the end of the game, toss all the debris. Everyone wins!

Give "door prizes" at family gatherings.

Whenever your family or friends come to your home for a get-together, offer a "door prize." Give away one or more things you no longer need or use to a lucky winner. If you wish, you can let guests select from several items or put a number of things in a "surprise" box. Get the kids involved, too—let them choose a few toys or games they've outgrown or don't play with anymore and add those to the array of prizes

Accomplish one clutter-clearing chore per day.

Make a to-do list and write down all the clutter-clearing tasks you intend to achieve. Then make a point of finishing at least one each day—even if it's just taking out the trash or returning borrowed books to the library. Break big chores down into smaller, manageable ones. The important thing is to see success. Continue working your way through your list until you've completed everything.

Spend ten minutes each day clearing clutter.

Make clutter-clearing a daily ritual and devote ten minutes each day to getting rid of clutter. Set a timer. Spend those ten minutes sorting through old magazines, tossing old cosmetics, culling business cards from your Rolodex—whatever you choose. When the timer goes off, stop. The beauty of this technique is that it keeps you from feeling overwhelmed by the task while helping you to incorporate clutter control into your daily routine.

Spend ten minutes each day putting stuff away.

When we're in a hurry, we tend to just dump stuff wherever we happen to be at the time—on kitchen counters, the coffee table, the floor, and so on. Allocate ten minutes each day to put stuff away in its proper place—set a timer if you wish. Hang up clothes, re-shelve books and CDs, pick up toys, put away dishes. Stop after the ten minutes are up. Once you fit this clutter-clearing task into your daily schedule, you may find you only need to spend ten minutes each morning or evening to keep your home tidy. And you won't waste time looking for stuff that isn't in its proper place.

**Every time you acquire something new,
get rid of something old.**

This rule applies to everything—clothes, toys, books, and CDs. If you throw out, recycle, or give away something each time you get something new, mathematics shows that your clutter can't increase.

Don't hold onto something just because you think it may become a valuable antique someday.

We've all read stories about someone netting a fortune for a piece of junk or seen an item—just like one we threw away!—selling for big bucks in an antique store. Although these lucky finds do turn up now and again, most junk is simply junk. If it doesn't have a purpose in your life now, don't hold onto it waiting for it to become valuable *someday*.

Toss old cards and letters.

Collector Isabella Stewart Gardner saved 7,000 letters from more than 1,000 correspondents (many of them famous names in history and the arts). But unless the cards and letters you receive have genuine value, either sentimental or monetary, don't hold onto this clutter. In some instances, old love letters can even create problems with new partners. Update your address book annually when you receive birthday, Christmas, or other holiday cards, then toss the cards and envelopes.

Get to know the Goodwill.

Find the location of the Goodwill or Salvation Army (or other charity that accepts drop-off goods) nearest you. Round up those old florists' vases, battered paperpacks, outgrown clothes and the like, bag them up, and drop them off. Try to keep a "Goodwill bag" going at all times: when it's full, drop it off and start the next one. Don't ask for a receipt unless you're really dropping off something valuable—and do not go inside the store. Just drop the bag at the back and go!

Set up a "swap shop" in your community.

The town next to mine has designated a shed next to the local dump as a community swap shop. People leave clothing, small appliances, books, and toys there for others to enjoy.

Check out www.freecycle.com.

This website is an international, grassroots effort to help people find new homes for stuff that's too good to just throw away. Part of a larger, nonprofit organization called RISE, it matches you up with people and organizations in your city who want what you no longer need. The only requirement is that everything must be free. It's a great way to help yourself and help others, too.

Don't go to flea markets and yard sales.

Many of us find it hard to pass up a bargain, even if we don't need it. My friend Harry, for instance, has a passion for yard sales. Whenever he comes to visit me in Massachusetts, he snaps up all sorts of terrific bargain items (last time he bought a mint-condition antique cast-iron sink for $10). Blinded by enthusiasm, he forgets that he'll have to ship his finds back to New Mexico where he lives. If you're the type who is easily tempted to buy something just because it's a good deal, avoid going to flea markets and yard sales. Instead of taking home another person's clutter, consider having your own yard sale to unload some of your old stuff.

Don't shop when you're upset or depressed.
Some people buy stuff as a way of making themselves feel better. Instead of going shopping when you feel bad, do something nice for yourself. Take a walk, get your nails done, enjoy a massage, have lunch with a friend, or see a funny movie.

Make household members aware of their clutter.
In her book *Organizing Plain & Simple*, Donna Smallin suggests putting colored peel-off stickers on items left lying around the house. Use a different color for each individual. Tagging clutter this way lets clutterers know to what extent they are contributing to the home's general messiness and may encourage them to change their behavior.

Make charitable contributions instead of buying more stuff for loved ones.

My friend Lyndsey has recently instituted a new gift-giving policy with her family and friends. Because everyone in her circle already has more stuff than they need, they have agreed to donate money to their favorite charities at Christmas, birthdays, and other special occasions, instead of buying each other material items. This practice has three benefits: it reduces clutter, helps those who are in need, and allows the giver a tax write-off.

Give "activity" gifts to loved ones.

Instead of giving friends and family members more stuff, treat them to a special activity; something they might not do for themselves, for instance. Take a loved one to a concert or play, out to dinner, on a trip to someplace he or she has always wanted to go. Or give them a little luxury: a massage, facial, or manicure. The two best gifts I ever received were a trip to Stonehenge and a hot-air balloon ride.

Pick up trash in your neighborhood.
We can all help to prevent clutter from piling up in our neighbor-hoods. When you go out for a walk, take a plastic bag along and pick up trash along the side of the road, on the beach, or in the woods.

Get rid of old electronics.
Holding onto that PC dinosaur (or three) in case your new one breaks? Give *yourself* a break and donate it to Goodwill or a charity that recycles them.

Establish a "lending network" with family and friends.

Create a personal "lending library" for books, CDs, DVDs, and videos. Circulate these among friends and family members. You may also wish to purchase other items, such as tools and equipment, in common. My friends Joel and Claire, for example, own a riding lawnmower jointly with their next-door neighbors, Carol and Dick. Sharing reduces costs, maintenance, and clutter. Everyone benefits.

If you haven't finished reading yesterday's paper, recycle it anyway.

Don't let "old news" clutter up your home. Even if you haven't finished reading yesterday's newspaper, recycle it—you probably won't miss anything important, and whatever you really need to know will likely be updated in today's publication.

Rotate your tchotchkes.

My friend Margaret's elderly mother had collected hundreds of tchotchkes over the years and allowed them to clutter every available surface in her home. Margaret tactfully explained that the sheer number of items made it difficult to really see and appreciate any of them. When her mother balked at getting rid of any of her memorabilia, Margaret suggested packing away about 90 percent in boxes and storing them in the garage. The other 10 percent were neatly displayed. Whenever her mother got tired of looking at the pieces on display, she could put them in the box and take out a few different tchotchkes. This system enabled her mother to enjoy her treasures anew.

Toss or fix broken stuff.

Are you holding on to broken articles that you keep meaning to repair, but never seem to get around to? If something has languished in its broken state in a closet, basement, or garage for more than a few months, either fix it or throw it away.

Wait three days to buy "impulse" items.

In Massachusetts, where I live, the law allows buyers three days to change their minds when making large purchases (such as houses and automobiles) and they can cancel the sale within that time period without penalty. You can implement a similar "buyer's remorse" strategy yourself to curb your own buying patterns. If you feel you can't live without something that's not really an essential, especially if it's a big-ticket item, give yourself three days to think it over before purchasing it. During the cooling-down period, you may discover you really don't want it as badly as you thought you did.

Decide whether you want to keep something before you put it away.

The best time to decide whether an item is worth keeping is before you put it away. Each time you pick up an article of questionable value, ask yourself if you really want/need it. If not, get rid of it right then and there.

Collect and contain stuff until you can put it away.

If you don't have time to put things away right now, collect odds and ends in a large container—a laundry basket, plastic milk crate, or rolling laundry bin works well—that you can carry or roll from room to room. As you make your way through your home, pick up items that don't belong in a particular room, toss them in the basket, and drop them off in their proper area. Later on, when you have more time, you can come back and finish the job, but at least you've taken the first step toward ordering your clutter by relocating it to the room where it belongs.

Use the 50 percent rule.

Pick an area in your home, such as the cabinet under the sink, the linen closet, or the west corner of the basement, and eliminate half of what's there. This may sound radical, but if you haven't sorted through these storage sites in a year or more, chances are you can easily get rid of a lot of stuff that's been stashed there and never miss it.

Store personal treasures in a "treasure chest."

Even the most inveterate unclutterer is likely to have some items that possess enough sentimental value to make them worth keeping. But you don't need to devote prime space in your home to these mementos. Pack them away in a personal "treasure chest." A wood, plastic, metal, or archival cardboard box will do. Then store it in an attic, garage, basement, or other out-of-the-way zone. Whenever you choose to take a trip down memory lane, open your treasure chest and enjoy looking at your loot.

Make one "to-do" list only.

Instead of keeping lists on your refrigerator, desk calendar, wall calendar, computer, and Day-Timer, plus Post-it notes stuck all over the place, combine everything you need to remember to do into a single list. Otherwise, you're likely to overlook something. Or you might not trust any of your lists and waste time checking all of them.

Invest in lots of organizing containers.

Many companies now make ingenious and practical storage containers for everything from shoes to soda to sporting goods. Treat yourself to lots of organizing goodies that make closets, cabinets, attics, basements, and other storage sites in your home more efficient.

> **TIP: Some containers come in attractive colors that let you organize stuff according to color—i.e., winter clothes in blue containers, summer ones in red.**

Keep it simple.

This slogan from Alcoholics Anonymous can be a good one to follow when it comes to keeping clutter under control. Approach clutter-clearing in a manner that is as stress-free as possible. Don't place unrealistic expectations on yourself or others; don't judge or blame yourself; accomplish tasks at your own pace; take it one step at a time.

Install shelves above doors and windows for displaying decorative objects.
The space above doors and windows usually goes untapped. Hang shelves above doors and windows, then display *objets d'art* and items you rarely use on them.

Give family heirlooms to your heirs now.
Instead of waiting to pass them along when she died, my grandmother gave family heirlooms and other treasures to her children and grandchildren while she was still alive. That way, she explained, she knew the items had gotten into the right hands and she could enjoy watching her loved ones' pleasure at receiving the prized possessions.

Reuse containers.

Some containers can be reused after they've served their initial purpose. To cut down on waste, recycle them and give them new life whenever possible. For instance, fancy fruit comes packaged in sturdy cardboard boxes with lots of sections that can be reused to hold arts and crafts supplies, workshop gadgets, small toys, and so on. Eyeshadow boxes with multiple color trays and sectioned vitamin boxes can be reused to keep earrings neat.

Never read junk mail.

Immediately toss all junk mail in the recycling bin or trash. Don't bother reading it or saving it.

Stop junk mail before it starts.

Contact companies and tell them you don't wish to receive their literature. Ask them to take you off their mailing lists. Ask companies you patronize not to share your information with other firms.

Cut down on catalogues.
When mail-order catalogues arrive, go through them and tear out pages that picture items you plan to order. If you aren't going to place the order right away, create a file for mail or phone orders and file only the pages you've selected. Don't keep the whole catalogue—recycle it immediately.

Become more socially conscious about what you buy.
Consider where something comes from before you buy it. Boycott items made by child labor, in sweatshops, or under conditions you don't find acceptable. Many people refuse to buy products that are tested on animals. Others prefer to purchase things made locally, rather than encouraging more jobs to be shipped off-shore. Express your beliefs with your pocketbook, and support companies who share your values.

Make a rule: Whoever makes the mess cleans it up.
If you continue to pick up after family members, they're unlikely to take responsibility for their own messes. Lay down the law: Whoever makes the mess, cleans it up. Pronto.

Reward yourself for a job well done.
Set a clutter-clearing goal. When you've reached it, reward yourself with a special treat (no, not a buying spree!). Rewarding yourself can be a great way to increase your motivation.

Never turn down an offer of help.
Don't think you have to do it all yourself, or that you are the only person who can do it right. When friends and family members offer to help, let them! In some cases, it may make sense to hire professional assistance.

Eliminate bad vibes.

What I call "energetic clutter" can have an adverse effect on you, even though you can't see it. Words, actions, emotions, and thoughts all create vibrations in the "energy grid" that surrounds us. Those vibes can linger in your home for a long time, causing stress, discord, and other unwanted feelings. Several methods can be used to clear the air: burn incense regularly; light a sage wand and waft the smoke through your rooms; spray citrus spritzer in each room; ring a bell in every room; sprinkle salt in the corners of your home. Make sure to open windows periodically, too, and let clean air circulate through your living space.

Versatile Storage Devices

Everyone has his or her own favorite storage solutions—here are some versatile clutter control devices you can use in just about any area of your home. All are inexpensive, easy to find, and immensely practical. Try them. You'll wonder how you ever lived without them!

• **Pegboards.** Great for hanging coats, hats, kids' clothes, towels, tools, necklaces, scarves, pots and pans, you name it. I like the wooden Shaker-style ones best.

• **Shoe caddies.** Shoes aren't the only things you can store in these lightweight, over-the-door hang-ups. Toys, tools, kitchen gadgets, artist supplies, and personal-care products all fit neatly into the convenient pockets. Canvas or plastic shoe caddies maximize storage space in any small area.

• **Baskets.** Attractive and lightweight, baskets come in all sizes and shapes. Often you can pick them up cheap at yard sales. Old-fashioned laundry baskets keep boots and shoes, sports equipment, and toys neatly contained. Small baskets are perfect for holding cosmetics, perfume, and personal-care items. A basket in your entryway keeps keys, glasses, and mail handy. Another advantage: You can carry baskets from room to room, if necessary.

• **Silverware trays.** Available in plastic, wicker, wood, and metal, silverware trays with divided compartments keep any drawer neat and orderly. Use them in a desk to hold pens, pencils, paper clips, staples, and other small office supplies. In a workshop drawer, they keep screwdrivers, pliers, and small tools handy. Artists will find them useful for storing brushes and tubes of paint. They're great for holding cosmetics, too.

• **Clear plastic boxes.** These come in lots of sizes and shapes, for storing everything from scarves and handkerchiefs to tax receipts to toys and outgrown baby clothes. Waterproof, clear, and easy to transport, you can see what's inside at a glance. Plastic boxes also protect items from potential damage due to moisture, insects, and dirt. Most are stackable, too.

Part Two

How to Take Back Control of Your Home (and Your Life)

CHAPTER 4

Exits and Entrances: Decks, Porches, Halls, Mudrooms, Doors, and More

Clear clutter from steps.

Clutter left on the stairs is not only unsightly, it can lead to accidents. Be scrupulous about clearing stuff from your steps, walkways, porches, and entrance areas—especially if elderly or impaired people will be using them.

Use a hall tree for hanging up backpacks.

Old-fashioned hall trees can be convenient places to hang back-packs, tote bags, purses, umbrellas, etc. Coats can then be hung over the bags, so hooks do double-duty. The trick is to make sure you hang stuff in an evenly distributed manner so the hall tree doesn't become unbalanced.

Hang Shaker-style pegboards for coats and hats.

The Shakers elevated neatness to an art form. These orderly people used pegboards for hanging clothing, cookware, tools, herbs, even chairs. Install attractive wooden pegboards in your entryway to hold coats, hats, and umbrellas. They're a great space-saving substitute if your hall or vestibule doesn't feature a closet.

Install hooks at "kid height."

Kids are more likely to hang up their gear if you position hooks at a height they can reach. Make it convenient for them.

Remove clutter from your entryway.

The outside of your home and its entrance are the first things visitors and passersby see. A cluttered entry gives others a poor first impression of you. Prevent clutter from accumulating here. Pick up trash from the sidewalk in front of your home; collect children's toys; rake leaves; and keep the grass and shrubs trimmed. Because the front of your home and its entrance symbolize your self-image, keeping it neat and orderly can help you enhance your own sense of self.

Label keys and hang them on a key board.

Old-fashioned butlers used to keep all the keys to the household neatly organized on key boards or in key cases hung on the wall. Each key would be labeled according to its purpose. You can use the same method to keep your household members' keys handy. Fasten a wooden plaque with small hooks on it near the entrance to your home. Beneath each hook, affix a label with the name of the person whose keys will hang there. Label keys to outbuildings and equipment, such as a boat or riding lawnmower, too.

Provide a convenient place for people to drop stuff upon entering your home.

Notice where people tend to drop stuff when they enter your home: It's often a kitchen counter, hall table, stairway, or even the floor! Make it easy for household members and visitors by providing a convenient place to put keys, glasses, and mail so they don't end up in a big pile. This could be a drawer located near the entryway, a basket or wooden box, even a cookie jar with a lid. Someone I know found an old-fashioned mannequin's hand, once used to display jewelry in a shop, and put it in her entryway—it made a humorous conversation piece and the fingers were perfect for holding key rings. Once you get accustomed to putting these items in the appropriate place, you won't waste time looking for them.

Use fabric-lined baskets for mittens and scarves.

Because knitted garments can get caught on wicker or rattan, choose fabric-lined baskets to hold woolly mittens, scarves, and hats. Or simply line a basket with a cotton dish towel to prevent snags and pulls.

Hang baskets, plastic buckets, bags, etc. from pegs to expand holding capacity.

You can extend the storage capacity of a pegboard by hanging baskets, canvas bags, plastic buckets, and other containers from the pegs. Containers such as these also allow you to hang up small stuff like keys and glasses, as well as mail and other articles that aren't designed for hanging.

Place a storage bench in your entryway.

Provide guests and household members a place to sit, so they can take off and put on boots or shoes comfortably. A bench can become a catch-all place to drop stuff, however, thereby defeating its purpose. A bench with a storage box under the seat is the ideal solution. The Victorians, whose homes were often short on closet space, had the right idea; they designed multipurpose hall pieces for storing gear that included a bench, chest, hooks, and mirror in a single, attractive unit.

Store recycling bins under the porch.

My friend Michael neatly stows his recycling bins under the back porch. A lattice-work screen between the porch deck and the ground keeps everything hidden from view, and a hinged door at the side allows him to toss bottles, cans, and plastic into the bins easily.

Use a plastic laundry tub or wicker laundry basket for storage.

Plastic laundry tubs or wicker laundry baskets provide a quick, convenient place to toss outdoor gear. Place one under a hall table to keep boots and skates neatly contained.

Retrofit dividers inside a trunk or foot locker.

To keep gear organized, make dividers out of wood and fit them into a trunk or foot locker to create two, three, or more compartments. Now boots and shoes stay neat, instead of ending up in a jumbled pile.

Use an old army foot locker or trunk for storage.

Metal trunks or foot lockers, like the ones soldiers used and kids took to camp, can be inexpensive storage solutions in an entryway. These durable containers provide space to stash boots, skates, and other bulky items, as well as a place to sit when you want to put on or take off footwear. Many foot lockers and trunks come fitted with removable trays where you can conveniently store gloves, hats, scarves, and other small stuff.

Place an armoire in your entryway.

If your entryway is large enough, place an armoire in it to store everything from coats and boots to magazines and newspapers awaiting recycling. Old-fashioned armoires (or wardrobes) were our ancestors' closets, and often feature interior hanging rods, drawers, shelves, and other handy storage options. These handsome cabinets add a decorative element in homes whose entrances open directly into the living room or a front hall.

Use a baker's rack for easy storage.
Baker's racks provide an attractive way to shelve stuff. Because these open units don't allow you to close the doors on clutter, however, you'll need to encourage household members to stash their stuff neatly. Place baskets, tins, bowls, boxes, bins, and other containers of various sizes on the shelves to expand the rack's utility and keep items such as gloves, keys, glasses, and hats organized and orderly.

Maximize corners in your entryway.
Don't waste valuable storage space in the corners of your entryway. Plastic corner shelf units designed to use in bathtub or shower stalls can be handy places to stash mittens, keys, sunglasses, and so on— especially if your area is small. These floor-to-ceiling systems are usually adjustable and made to maximize utility while occupying as little space as possible.

Dry wet mittens on a wine rack.
An accordion wine rack quickly converts to a convenient drying rack for mittens, gloves, caps, and other small items. Hang one in your entryway in the wintertime, then in warm weather fold it away (or use it as it was intended—to hold wine).

Hang a shoe caddy on the door.
Expand the space in a hall closet by hanging a canvas or plastic shoe caddy inside the door. These inexpensive units are perfect for holding gloves, glasses, keys, and other small items. If you don't have a hall closet in your entryway, you can hang a shoe caddy on the inside of your front door to keep stuff neat and convenient.

Put a chest with lots of drawers in your entry area.
Chests with lots of drawers are great for storing outdoor gear. Use small drawers for keys and glasses, larger ones for hats, scarves, and mittens. Give each member of the household a drawer to store stuff.

CHAPTER 5

Dirty Little Secrets: Bathrooms

Use a basket to keep toiletries for guests neat and convenient.
Here's a pleasant and convenient way to make guests feel welcome in your home. Arrange sample-sized soap, shampoo, lotion, rolled-up hand towels, and other personal-care items in individual baskets for your guests. Keep one or more toiletry baskets stocked and handy, so you are always ready when guests come to visit overnight.

Use cleaning products that do "double duty."

Instead of buying a lot of different, specialized cleaning products, choose cleansers that can be used for a variety of jobs. Whenever possible, choose "green" cleaners in recycled containers that don't contribute to environmental pollution.

Clear clutter in the bathroom to enhance your health.

As mentioned in Chapter 2, the bathroom is linked symbolically with health. From the perspective of feng shui, cleaning and uncluttering your bathroom can help your body to purify itself on a physical and emotional level.

Use a basket to hold extra rolls of toilet paper.

Keep extra rolls of toilet paper neat and handy in a decorative basket, and set it near the toilet. (Each time you refill the toilet-paper holder from the basket, remember to replace the roll.)

Place guest towels in an accordion wine rack.
Hand towels stay neat if you roll them up and put them in the sections of a wine rack.

Put a cutlery tray in a vanity drawer.
Trays designed to hold silverware are perfect containers for personal-care items, too. In a bathroom vanity drawer, they keep cosmetics, combs and brushes, toothpaste and toothbrushes, and other small items neat.

Install hooks or pegs on the back of the door for towels.
If your bathroom doesn't have enough places to hang wet towels, affix hooks or pegs to the back of the door. Make sure to install some at kid-height.

Dry tiles after each shower.
To prevent mildew and mold from building up in your tub/shower area—and to keep grout from getting gross—wipe tiles dry with a bath towel or sponge after every shower. Tiles stay clean and sparkling longer and require less care overall.

Buy assortment packs of tampons.
Rather than purchasing several boxes of different-sized tampons, choose packages that offer an assortment.

Reduce clutter in your medicine cabinet.
Think of your bathroom's medicine cabinet as prime real estate. Only store things you use every day—toothbrushes and toothpaste, makeup, hairbrush, and so on— in this space. Larger items and things you use less often, such as cleaning supplies, healthcare remedies, and specialty bath products, can go in the cabinet under the sink or in a linen closet.

Apply the 50 percent rule to your medicine cabinet.

At least once a year, empty your entire medicine cabinet. Wash and dry the shelves. Sort through the contents and eliminate medications whose shelf life has expired. Dump everything you haven't used in the past year. Get rid of duplicate cosmetics. Relocate items that you don't use every day to another spot. Your end goal is to reduce medicine-cabinet clutter by half.

Group products into categories.

Organizing bathroom items into categories makes it easier to find what you want when you want it. Plus, you can see at a glance whether you already have enough bubble bath, cough medicine, or bandages, so you don't accidentally buy something you don't need. Arrange cleaning products together in one area, cosmetics in another, first-aid items in another, and so on. Position things you use most often in front, seasonal or infrequently used ones behind.

Use hanging wire baskets for personal-care products.
Shower and bath needs stay handy when collected in wire baskets. Rather than lining up shampoo, soap, and other items along the tub rim, corral them in one convenient place. Open mesh baskets allow sponges and soap to dry properly, without leaving a gunky residue on the tub.

Hang bath items from a towel bar.
Keep shampoo, conditioner, soap, sponges, and other bath and shower gear neat and handy by hanging them up. Install a towel bar above your tub, then use shower curtain hooks to hang small wire mesh or plastic baskets from the bar. Corral all the stuff that usually clutters the rim of your tub in the baskets.

Give your bathroom a daily sweeping.
It's easy to give your bathroom a quick sweeping up if you keep a dustpan and whisk broom handy. This simple chore takes only a couple of minutes and will help your bathroom look tidy.

When in doubt, throw it out.
Medicines and cosmetics have a limited shelf-life. Check the dates on medications and get rid of them when they reach their expiration dates. Many cosmetics start to lose their effectiveness after six months or so. If you aren't sure if something is still usable, toss it.

Store bath products in clear plastic boxes.
Once you've organized your toiletries, cleaning products, and health-related items into categories, group them into clear plastic boxes that can stack under your bathroom sink. These boxes maximize your available storage space, protect objects from moisture, and keep like items with like so you can find them easily.

Corral cosmetics in specially designed organizing containers.
Lots of tiny tubes, tins, and jars can really clutter up your bathroom cabinets and waste valuable space. Treat yourself to clear plastic containers that are specially designed to hold lipsticks, mascara, nail polish, and eye shadows. Opt for configurations that make the most of height so you maximize the amount of available space on the shelves of your medicine cabinet or bathroom vanity.

Corral personal-care items into coffee mugs.
We all have extra, unmatched coffee mugs we don't use for coffee. Put them to work in your bathroom, where they make ideal containers for all sorts of personal items. Use one for toothbrushes, another for cosmetic brushes, another for Q-tips, another for nail files and polish, another for cotton balls, and so on.

Install a towel shelf above the tub.
Many bathtub surrounds stop short of the ceiling. If this is the case in your bathroom, install a shelf above the surround and stack extra towels on it. This frees up space in your linen closet and keeps towels handy.

Keep the toilet bowl shining.
Use denture cleaning tablets to remove stains from porcelain in the toilet bowl and keep it sparkling clean.

> **TIP: My friend Kathleen, who lightens her hair to Marilyn Monroe blonde, recommends dumping any leftover bleach in the toilet to remove stains.**

CHAPTER 6

Eating It Up: Kitchens

Think of your kitchen in terms of work zones.

Assess your kitchen space according to the tasks you perform in certain areas—preparation, cooking, and cleanup, for instance. Store and arrange items you use for each of these tasks in the zone where they will be utilized. For example, knives and mixing bowls should be placed in the preparation zone instead of near the stove.

Unclutter your kitchen to enhance your health.

As discussed in Chapter 2, the kitchen is associated with nutrition and health because this is where meals are prepared. Symbolically, cleaning and uncluttering your kitchen can have a positive effect on your health and encourage you to pay more attention to eating a nutritious diet.

Toss items that are missing pieces.

Empty your cabinets completely and assess the contents with a critical eye. Toss anything that can no longer be used because it doesn't have all its pieces, such as plastic containers without lids.

Get rid of unnecessary gadgets.

How many "time-saving" gadgets do you have in your kitchen? How many of them do you actually use? If electric bread makers, hotdog bun warmers, and electric carving knives aren't earning their keep, get rid of them.

Create a convenient breakfast area.

Most of us are in a hurry—and maybe half asleep—when we're fixing breakfast. Make it easy on yourself. Place everything you need for breakfast in one spot in the kitchen—the coffeemaker and coffee, toaster, butter dish, jam jars, cereal bowls, and utensils.

Store dishes on open shelves instead of in cabinets.

If you are re-designing your kitchen, consider installing open shelving to hold the dishes and glassware you use daily. This arrangement is not only more convenient, it gives your kitchen an airy appearance and can make a small space seem larger.

Attach wire racks under shelves.

An easy way to expand the storage space in your cabinets is to install wire racks to the bottoms of shelves. Store small items here that might otherwise get lost in the back of your cabinets.

Install pull-out trays in base cabinets.

Pull-out trays on rollers make it easy to access pots, pans, skillets, and other kitchen equipment that might otherwise languish at the back of your base cabinets. They also make it easier to get at bulky and heavy cookware.

Use an armoire in your kitchen.

Our ancestors used armoires to hold clothing, but if your kitchen is large enough, consider using one to house pots and pans, cookbooks, kitchen appliances, and lots of other stuff, too. These roomy and attractive wardrobes can be outfitted with shelves, hooks, dividers—whatever you need to neatly organize your kitchen equipment—and conceal it behind closed doors.

Only keep a few favorite cookbooks.

Most of us have more cookbooks than we regularly use. Some may only contain a couple of recipes we like. Go through your collection, get rid of the ones you rarely consult, and only save your favorites.

Store cookbooks away from the kitchen.

If your kitchen is small, you may not want to allocate precious cabinet space for cookbooks. Instead, house them in bookshelves in another room. Keep only the ones you use weekly (or more often) in your kitchen.

Check out cookbooks from your local library.

Libraries often stock an interesting selection of cookbooks that you might not be able to justify owning, but would enjoy using periodically. Instead of buying specialty or novelty cookbooks, borrow them from your local library.

Put your favorite recipes on index cards or the computer.
Instead of taking up shelf space with cookbooks, copy your favorite recipes onto index cards and house them in a card file box. If you prefer, you can create your own collection of favorite recipes in a loose-leaf binder. Or make a file in your computer for recipes.

Laminate favorite recipes and hang them up.
Get your favorite and frequently used recipes laminated, then put them on a key ring and hang them on a hook near your preparation area.

> **TIP:** Use different-colored index cards to color-key recipes for easy identification: pink for meat, green for veggies, yellow for grains, etc.

Toss spices after six months.

Spices start to loss their potency after a few months. Don't clutter up your cabinets with old spices; throw them away after about six months.

Keep a small bottle of olive oil out and replenish it regularly.

If you use olive oil to cook with, buy it in bulk (it's cheaper), but store the large containers in a closet or cabinet. Place an attractive, smaller oil bottle near the stove and refill it as needed from the large container.

> **TIP: Group oil, vinegar, salt and pepper, and frequently used condiments on a tray with handles, so you can easily transport them to the table.**

Rotate food in your pantry.

When my father died in 1991, he still had cans of K-rations left over from World War II in his kitchen closet! How long have your canned goods, boxes of pasta and rice, and jars of preserves and relishes been sitting in your pantry? Rotate items periodically, so older ones get used up. When you purchase food products, position the newer ones behind similar items that have been languishing on your shelves for a while.

Rotate food in your freezer.

Even though scientists have discovered prehistoric woolly mammoths well-preserved in the icy arctic regions, frozen food doesn't last forever. Rotate food in your freezer periodically. Move items that are nearing their expiration dates to the front of your freezer so you remember to use them up promptly. Put newly purchased items underneath or behind similar ones. At least twice a year, clean out your freezer and organize its contents.

Store onions in pantyhose.
My friend Susan came up with this novel idea to prevent onion skins from crumbling and littering the vegetable drawers in your refrigerator or pantry: Store onions in the legs of pantyhose. Cut off the legs of old pantyhose, slide onions inside, and fasten with a twist tie.

Hang cutting boards.
If you have several cutting boards, you can keep them handy yet out of the way by hanging them on the insides of lower cabinet doors.

Set aside one "clutter drawer" in your kitchen.
No matter how orderly and organized you are, you're bound to have some stuff that just doesn't seem to fit anywhere. Designate one drawer or bin in your kitchen for miscellaneous clutter. Once a month, sort through your clutter drawer and get rid of anything you no longer need.

File coupons according to expiration date.

Index card boxes are perfect for filing coupons. So are accordion files. Use the tab dividers to organize coupons according to category, such as cereal, pet food, and cleansers. Within each category, arrange coupons by expiration date, with the oldest coupons at the front, so you remember to use them before they become outdated.

Don't save lots of plastic bags.

You'll get more plastic shopping bags every time you go to the supermarket, so don't bother saving more than a few. Many stores have places to recycle excess plastic bags.

Use a plastic dish pan to corral cleaning supplies.

A plastic dish pan will keep sponges, detergent, scrub brushes and pads, and other cleaning supplies neat and convenient under your sink. It also prevents wet items and drips from making a mess in your cabinet.

Keep plastic trash bags neat and handy.

One of my editors, Delilah Smittle, has discovered that a tall basket with a lid makes an ideal storage place for both plastic trash bags and daily trash. She recommends placing extra bags in the bottom of the basket. Line a small trash can with a plastic bag, set it on top of the extra bags, and close the basket's lid. Each day, throw out the trash and replace the old plastic bag with a new one from the bottom of the basket.

Arrange your shopping list according to the supermarket's floor plan.

If you always shop at the same supermarket, you probably know the floor plan pretty much by heart. You'll save time by writing your shopping list in the same order as the store organizes its items. You can select what you need the first time through the store and won't have to double back for things you missed.

Collect loose change in film canisters.

Plastic film canisters are perfect for holding coins. Organize loose change by denomination instead of mixing nickels, dimes, and quarters. You can quickly grab a canister to take the laundromat or keep a few in your car for parking meters and tolls.

Don't buy readily available items in bulk.

Unless you're feeding a large family, it probably doesn't pay to purchase items such as pasta, resealable plastic storage bags, or aluminum foil in bulk. You may save a bit overall, but you'll sacrifice space in your kitchen or pantry storing these products. A friend of mine came from the "be prepared" school and always kept plenty of everything on hand, so he'd never run out. When he moved to another part of the country, he gave me his unopened containers of freezer bags, paper towels, and olive oil. A year and a half later, I still haven't used up all the stuff he left behind.

Hang lightweight objects on a folding screen.
Instead of letting them take up room in a drawer or cabinet, hang bulky, lightweight items such as sieves and molds on hooks and attach them to a tri-fold screen. This technique can serve another purpose, too. Position the screen so it hides something unattractive such as the trash can or recycling bins, a clunky architectural feature or plumbing element.

Hang pots and pans on a metal pipe.
Decorative wrought iron or wooden hanging racks are great for keeping pots and pans conveniently out of the way when they're not in use. But an ordinary piece of copper pipe works just as well and is much less expensive. Purchase a length of pipe from the hardware store and hang it from the ceiling or position it between two walls, cabinets, and so on. Use S-hooks to hang pots and pans on the pipe.

Hang mops and brooms.

If closet space in your kitchen is limited, hang mops, brooms, the ironing board, and other tall items on the inside of a door. It needn't be a door in your kitchen—a basement or garage door might work just as well. Use hooks or specially designed hanging units to keep these items out of the way yet convenient.

Hang spray bottles on a rod or hooks.

Make more use of under-the-sink cabinet space by attaching hooks or a rod near the upper part of the cabinet. Hang up spray bottles and other items so you can store other stuff in the bottom part of the cabinet.

Store dry pet food in plastic containers.

After you open a bag or box of dry pet food, transfer the contents to a plastic container with a lid. Not only will this keep the food fresher longer, it helps prevent spillage.

Corral dishwashing tools in flowerpots.

Small porcelain flowerpots are convenient and attractive containers for holding scrubbing brushes, scrapers, sponges, steel wool, and other dishwashing equipment.

De-clutter cleaning supplies.

Evaluate your cleaning products regularly and get rid of any that have dried up or otherwise outlived their usefulness. For instance, there's no good reason to hold onto partly used steel wool pads or old cans of scouring powder that will leave messy rust stains in your cabinet.

Store lightweight items in wicker baskets.

Plastic containers, microwave goodies, and other lightweight, unbreakable items can be tossed in an open wicker basket instead of taking up room in a kitchen cabinet. Lay a colorful dish towel over the basket to protect the contents from dust and cover up the clutter.

Put place mats and napkins in an accordion wine rack.

If drawer space is limited in your kitchen or dining room, consider rolling up place mats and napkins and storing them in an accordion wine rack. They'll stay neat and convenient, leaving drawers free for other articles.

Install half-depth shelves in kitchen cabinets.

Maximize the amount of storage space available in your kitchen cabinets by installing half-depth shelves at the back. Mugs, small bowls, glassware, vases, and other narrow items can be placed here, leaving the main shelves for plates and larger dishes.

Store spices in an old medicine cabinet.

Attractive wall-hung, antique medicine cabinets are perfect for housing spices. The small shelves are the right size for most spice jars and tins, and you can close the door to hide the containers and keep them from getting dusty.

Protect your pots and pans.

If you stack pots and pans in cabinets, keep them from getting damaged—especially the non-stick ones—by putting paper towels between them.

Keep a small selection of tools in your kitchen.

Keep a set of tools you use frequently—screwdriver, hammer, pliers, scissors—handy in a box or drawer in your kitchen. You won't have to make a trip to the shed or basement each time a small repair job arises. And if tools are close at hand, you're more likely to take care of repairs promptly.

Organize odds and ends in soap dishes.

Odds and ends, such as safety pins, twist ties, and thumb tacks, will stay orderly if you corral them in china or plastic soap dishes. Place a variety of soap dishes in a drawer to keep all that little stuff from sliding around.

CHAPTER 7

Media Control: Family Rooms

Get stuff off the floor first.
If you don't have time to do a thorough pick up right away, at least collect the stuff that's scattered on the floor. Stash everything in a laundry basket, large box, or trash bag until you can deal with it properly. Your home will look neater instantly.

Divide your family room into activity zones.

If your family room is used for a variety of purposes by a number of household members, divide it into sections or "activity zones." Organize the space by putting everything and only things that relate to a particular activity in its designated area. For instance, keep books, newspapers, and magazines in the reading area; CDs, DVDs, videos, and remotes in the entertainment area; children's games and toys in a play area, and so on.

Unclutter your family room to improve family relationships.

As discussed in Chapter 2, the family room is the heart of your home and the place where household members come together to interact. Therefore, uncluttering this area can have a positive, symbolic effect on relationships between family members. Removing clutter helps to reduce stress and clear up confusion that may be disturbing the harmony in your home life. Making a commitment to put your family room in order shows you are committed to improving your relationships with loved ones.

Unclutter your family room to improve your social life.

The family room is also the place where you entertain guests, so it symbolizes your social life. Removing clutter from this area can help attract friends and clear up tensions or obstacles that may have been impeding positive social relationships. A neat, orderly living room makes visitors feel welcome and comfortable in your home, psychologically and physically.

Corral remotes in a basket.

Are you always hunting for the remote? Corral all your remotes in a convenient basket near your entertainment area, and remember to put them back in the basket when you've finished using them.

Cull videos and DVDs annually.

The same once-a-year clearing plan goes for videos and DVDs, too. If you aren't going to watch them again, pass them along to someone who will enjoy them.

Out with the old magazines, in with the new.
When the new issue of a magazine arrives, get rid of the old one. Keep a box or bag handy for magazines you plan to recycle to friends, doctors' offices, nursing homes, laundromats, and so on.

Share books and magazines.
Take books and magazines you aren't going to read again to nursing homes, hospitals, homeless shelters, and laundromats to share with others.

Save only magazine pictures and articles.
Advertising makes up most of a magazine. Instead of holding onto the entire magazine, cut out pictures and articles that interest you and that you think you might want to refer to again. Organize them in a scrapbook or binder according to subject. Then recycle the rest of the magazine. You'll not only reduce clutter, you'll save time looking for that special photo, information, recipe, or idea in the future.

Organize books by subject and author.
If you organize books according to their subject matter, then alphabetize them by author, you'll be able to find the one you want quickly. Another effective method is to arrange books you use often—reference books, for instance—at eye level. Put those you want to keep, but won't read frequently, on the topmost shelves.

Cull books annually.
At least once a year, go through your books and eliminate the ones you probably won't read again. Recycle them to friends or relatives, donate them to your local library or senior center, or sell them at a yard sale.

Straighten piles of books and magazines.
If you don't have time to shelve books and magazines, at least straighten them. They won't look as messy if their edges are aligned and the piles are neat.

Eliminate curtains and drapes.

Curtains and drapes collect dust, block light, and can make a room seem smaller. Instead, use narrow blinds or shades when privacy is desired or to reduce light. If privacy isn't an issue, eliminate window treatments altogether and let the sun shine in.

Use a trunk for a coffee table.

Instead of a standard coffee table, use a large wooden trunk in front of your sofa. Now your "table" does double duty, providing storage as well as a surface for glasses, books, and magazines.

Decorate with small chests of drawers or cabinets.

Instead of end tables, decorate with small chests of drawers or cabinets that provide storage space as well as an extra surface. Perfect for keeping books, remotes, and glasses convenient and out of sight when they're not in use.

File slides and negatives in plastic sleeves.

Keep photographic negatives and slides protected and orderly by slipping them into plastic "sleeves." Sheets of plastic negative holders can be organized in three-ring binders for safekeeping. Arrange by date, subject, project, trip, or any other method that makes it easy for you to locate the pictures you want.

> **TIP: Professional photographers make contact sheets that show miniature prints of each photo on a roll. This technique enables you to spot the pictures you like best when it comes time to print or enlarge them.**

House entertainment equipment in an armoire.

Large, decorative armoires or wardrobes aren't just for the bedroom—they make attractive and useful storage additions to your family room, too. These versatile cabinets can be used to house television and stereo equipment, computers, books, CDs—just about anything.

Place cacti on windowsills.

In her book *Cut the Clutter and Stow the Stuff*, Lori Baird recommends setting prickly cacti on windowsills to discourage family members from dropping clutter there. After getting stuck a few times, they usually get the message.

Keep a laundry basket handy for quick pick ups.

If you don't have time to pick up and put away clutter at the end of the day or when guests drop in unexpectedly, stash everything in a laundry basket and hide it until you can do a thorough job.

Replace a wood stove with one that burns gas.

Wood-burning stoves may be romantic, but they are also messy. Reduce your cleaning chores by replacing a wood stove with a gas-burning one. You won't waste time sweeping up wood chips and ashes. Gas-fired stoves tend to be more efficient, safe, and easy to regulate, too.

Highlight your treasures.
As feng shui consultant Jami Lin wrote in an article for *New Age Retailer* magazine, "The less clutter you have, the more your favorite items can be featured." When your living space is jam-packed with stuff, the treasures may get lost among the trash and trivia. Pruning away the excess detritus will allow you to show off your special pieces to best advantage.

Maximize wall height.
Install floor-to-ceiling bookshelves or wall systems to make the most of wall height. Adjustable shelving is a must, of course; drawers and cabinets a plus. Try to combine as much as possible into your wall storage system, such as books, electronics, and *objets d'art*. Opt for flexibility, so if your needs change you won't have to replace the entire arrangement.

Turn a wall into a picture library.

You don't have to limit yourself to one or two pictures on a wall. Frame lots of your favorite photographs in matching frames, then hang them artfully so they pretty much cover an entire section of a wall. Position artwork so that the center of the arrangement is approximately at eye level. Don't hang them halfway between the floor and ceiling or between the ceiling and the back of the sofa. This technique is especially good for displaying small pictures or photos that would seem skimpy if hung on a wall by themselves.

Plan your picture wall first.

Before you start hammering nails into your walls, cut paper rectangles the size of your framed pictures and tape them in place. This lets you see what the finished arrangement will look like and you can rearrange the papers easily. Or draw the entire configuration to scale on graph paper.

Create a "message area" in your family room.

To be certain you don't miss important messages, organize an area for taking, writing down, and retrieving messages. Provide a blackboard, bulletin board, note pad, and plenty of pens and pencils. Train family members in that most basic of secretarial arts—answering the phone.

> **TIP: You may find it helpful to use professional message pads with carbon copies to make sure a name or number isn't lost.**

CHAPTER 8

Private, Keep Out: Bedrooms

Do away with over-the-dresser mirrors.

Most women put on makeup in the bathroom, rather than the bedroom, and don't get much use out of the conventional mirror hung above the dresser. Eliminate this bedroom accessory and hang a full-length mirror on the back of a door. This option is more practical and efficient: Now you can maximize the wall space above the dresser by installing shelves, cabinets, or other storage pieces instead.

Store extra linens under the bed.

Even though feng shui's tenets advise against storing stuff under the bed, in a small home this space seems too good to waste. If you don't have room in a linen closet for extra sheets and pillowcases, store them in a box under the bed. Suitcases are good containers for storing linens and blankets, too.

Don't let dirty laundry collect in your bedroom.

Dirt, disorder, and cast-off stuff in the master bedroom symbolizes discord or disappointments in a romantic relationship. Put dirty clothes in a hamper as soon as you take them off—don't let laundry clutter up your bedroom where it can clutter up your love life.

Utilize height in a small bedroom.

If wall or floor space is limited in a bedroom, think vertical. Maximize your storage area by using tall chests of drawers or armoires instead of horizontal dressers.

Corral loose change.

Instead of emptying your pockets and leaving loose change on the dresser top, choose a special "money jar" for holding coins. Put the jar near your home's most-used entrance. Each time you come in or go out, drop one (or more) coins in the money jar. As you do this, repeat an affirmation such as "This coin now multiplies itself ten times" and imagine money flowing to you. This easy feng shui "cure" helps attract prosperity.

Unclutter the master bedroom to improve romantic relationships.

As mentioned in Chapter 2, the master bedroom symbolizes intimacy and romantic relationships. Clutter in this room can lead to tension, confusion, and discord between you and a partner. By cleaning up your bedroom, you demonstrate a willingness to clear away problems that may have been keeping you from enjoying a happy love life.

Decorate with antique medicine cabinets.

Antique wooden medicine cabinets are attractive and convenient places to store eyeglasses, watches, cosmetics, and other small stuff. Instead of letting these articles clutter up your night stand, stash them in an old oak or pine cabinet hung on the wall in your bedroom.

> **TIP: Many of these medicine cabinets have mirrors on their doors. Or, you can affix a picture on the cabinet door. Consider hanging the medicine cabinet in the space above the dresser, where the mirror used to be. You can even group several to create an interesting wall arrangement.**

Remove work-related materials from your bedroom.

Make a clear distinction between areas for rest and areas for work. This is especially important if you live in a small apartment. Don't let paperwork, computers, and other work-related materials get a foothold in your sleeping quarters, where their presence may interfere with your rest.

Choose neutral-colored bed linens.

Colorful, patterned sheets and comforters may be fun, but decorating with a neutral color palette offers more flexibility. If you use basics such as white, ivory, or sage instead, you can easily switch linens from one bedroom to another as necessary. Going back to basics lets you cut down on the number of linens you keep on hand and frees up closet space.

Use mesh bags for dirty socks.
Here's a convenient way to keep socks from disappearing in the laundry. Put them in mesh bags when you take them off. To keep socks from getting mixed up, give each member of the household his or her own mesh bag and affix the person's name to it. If you really want to make sure socks don't go missing, pin mates together when you take them off before tossing them in the bag.

Rotate socks and undergarments.
Socks and undergarments will wear evenly if you rotate them. After washing, fold socks and undies and arrange them in your drawer so that the most recently worn ones are on the bottom of the pile. Take clean items from the top.

Store canned goods under the bed.

This may not be the most convenient storage option, but in a small apartment you need to utilize every possibility. When my mother was in her "survivalist phase," she stored extra canned goods and paper products she'd set aside in case of a catastrophe under the beds.

Keep scarves neat in plastic boxes.

Slippery silk scarves can slide around and get messy in a dresser drawer. Instead of just stacking them, fold them and store them in a clear plastic box with a lid so they stay organized and neatly pressed until you are ready to wear them.

Use a novel as a doorstop.

My writer friend Kate has a lovely summer home in Maine. But like many old houses, its floors aren't completely level. She uses hefty, hardcover novels as doorstops during the day. If someone wants to read before falling asleep, they'll find a good book close at hand.

Polish shoes regularly.
This task not only keeps your shoes looking their best, it reminds you how many pairs you actually own—and which ones you haven't worn lately. To cut down on polishing and free up space in your closet, take the shoes you rarely wear to a consignment shop.

Store off-season clothes in suitcases.
Suitcases take up a lot of room. Utilize all that empty space inside them to store off-season clothing. Because suitcases seal tightly, moths and other insects can't get inside to damage your garments, so they are good places to keep sweaters and blankets.

Arrange socks, pantyhose, and accessories by color.
If you organize socks, pantyhose, scarves, and other accessories by color, you'll save time dressing and packing for trips. Another plus: You can see at a glance how many items you have of a particular color, so you won't run out of a color you need or buy more than you need of another color.

CHAPTER 9

Battle Stations: Kids' Rooms

Divide children's rooms into zones.

Kids' rooms stay neater and easier to manage if you divide them into "activity zones"—sleeping, play, homework, and so on. Place everything related to school, such as the desk, computer, and books, in one area; toys, games, and sports equipment in another section of the room; and so on.

Unclutter children's rooms to improve their self-confidence and identity.

Clutter symbolizes stress, confusion, and instability. As discussed in Chapter 2, clearing up clutter in children's rooms can improve their sense of security and help bolster their self-confidence. Just as removing graffiti from parks and schools has been shown to improve children's self-images and sense of well-being, removing messiness in their rooms can have a beneficial impact on their identities, too.

Unclutter children's rooms to enhance focus and direction.

Reducing clutter in kids' rooms can also help them to focus better and may have a positive effect on such problems as Attention Deficit Disorder. By cleaning and organizing their rooms, children learn to focus on goals and accomplish tasks. Putting their rooms in order symbolically shows they are putting their lives in order, too.

Don't buy kids stuff just to keep them quiet.
The practice of buying kids things as bribes to keep them quiet practically guarantees that you'll end up with unwanted clutter. It also sends undesirable messages to children.

Corral toys in a hammock.
A mesh hammock, hung in the corner of a kid's bedroom, makes a great container for toys. Kids can toss toys into the hammock when they've finished playing with them, and can easily see through the holes to locate a favorite toy.

Store toys in a door-hung shoe caddy.
Shoe caddies designed to hang on a door provide lots of convenient storage for stuffed animals, dolls, and other small toys. Kids can easily stash toys in the individual pockets and keep their stuff neatly organized. Close the door to contain the clutter and keep it out of sight.

Store small toys in decorative boxes.

This clutter-clearing tip has an additional "plus": It encourages kids to be creative. Collect boxes in various sizes and shapes—shoe boxes, round hat boxes, or wine boxes— in which kids can sort and store toys. Save sturdy mailing boxes that are in good shape, too. Shoe boxes can be used to contain toy cars and other small items. Hat boxes can be pretty places to store doll clothes. Wine boxes with dividers might hold arts and craft supplies. Let children decorate the boxes with magazine pictures, drawings, photographs, and other images they find attractive and that relate to what's inside the boxes. Because the decorated boxes express their own ideas and imaginations, kids are more likely to use them to hold toys and keep them organized.

Stuff pajamas into a throw pillow cover.

Use a child's pajamas to make a throw pillow. Give each child his or her own decorative cover—pjs stay neatly contained during the day and are convenient at bedtime.

Contain shoes in a large basket.
Make it easy for kids to keep their shoes from littering the floor by providing each child with an oversized shoe basket. Old-fashioned laundry baskets make attractive storage bins into which kids of all ages can toss sneakers, sandals, and boots so they are neatly contained.

Stash toys in a trash can.
Colorful plastic trash cans with lids make ideal storage containers for toys, too. When play time is finished, kids can toss toys into the trash can and put the lid on clutter. In a household with more than one child, give each child a different-colored trash can to store his or her toys.

Store extra sheets in children's closets.
If you don't have adequate storage space in a linen closet, give children their own bed linens to store in their closets.

Use sleeping bags for kids' sleepovers.

Kids don't need to have an extra guest bed for their friends. Sleeping bags can be fun for kids to use for sleepovers—and they're easy to store under the bed or in a closet when not in use. Using sleeping bags cuts down on linens and laundry, too.

Collect toys in rolling laundry hampers.

Canvas laundry bins on aluminum frames with wheels also make great storage spots for kids' toys. When it's time to clean up, kids can roll the bins around their rooms and quickly toss games, stuffed animals, and other toys into the canvas container, then tuck the whole thing into a closet or corner.

Organize kids' artwork.

Give children three-ring binders to hold their artwork and make it easy to view. Date their drawings—it's fun to look back and chronicle a child's development by his or her drawings.

Keep infants' toys to a minimum.

Infants can become overstimulated by clutter. Limit toys and para-phernalia to a few soft, cuddly stuffed animals that will give a baby comfort and security, without creating confusion.

Give kids their own baskets for personal-care items.

A basket with a handle is perfect for holding hairbrushes, combs, barrettes, nail polish, and other personal-care items. Children can toss all their personal articles in the baskets and conveniently carry them from bedroom to bathroom.

Schedule time for kids to clean their rooms.

Set a time each week when kids are expected to clean their rooms. Schedule this "appointment" just as you would a soccer game or trip to the dentist. It's easier to get children to clean up when they have a regular routine in place.

Give kids "Roundabout Roller" units for storage.

Inexpensive "Roundabout Roller" storage caddies are composed of several drawers stacked in a lightweight aluminum frame that's perfect for storing toys, books, hobby supplies, hair brushes, and so on. Wheels allow kids to roll the unit around easily. Brightly colored drawers offer kids the option of organizing their stuff by category. Or several kids can stash stuff in a single unit, each using his or her own color-coded drawers.

Install shelves in kids' closets.

Open shelves provide a convenient place for kids to stash stuff. The key is to install shelves at "kid height" and make them adjustable, so as the child grows or his/her collection of gear changes, you can reposition the shelves easily.

Install shelves above windows and doors in kids' rooms.
Affix a shelf above each window and doorway in a child's room for displaying toys or treasures that aren't used on a regular basis—or items that the child may not be old enough yet to enjoy and take care of properly (such as antique dolls or old train sets). Periodically, rearrange the displayed items to keep the room looking fresh and interesting.

Organize kids' closets a couple of weeks before school starts.
The end of summer, just before school starts, is the perfect time to clean out kids' closets. Pass on clothing that children don't wear or have outgrown to siblings, friends, or charity, or take lightly worn items to a consignment shop. Keep a list of the items you've decided to keep, so when you shop for back-to-school clothes you know what to buy.

Use stackable plastic boxes for art supplies.
Clear plastic containers with lids are ideal for holding crayons, paints, markers, and other art supplies. Kids can see what's inside, but you may also want to label the containers. If something spills, it won't drip onto furnishings, and you can wash the plastic container easily.

Pack traveling essentials in a special gym bag or backpack.
In joint-custody arrangements, make it easy for everyone by keeping a special bag or backpack filled with the things that each child needs to take with him/her from one place to another.

Photograph kids' projects.
You may be able to avoid storing many of your kids' projects if you photograph them instead. Keep a photo album rather than hanging on to the projects themselves.

Store kids' artwork in cardboard tubes.

Artists roll up artwork and slide it into cardboard tubes to protect it from damage. You can store children's pictures the same way—reuse the cardboard tubes from wrapping paper, paper towels, plastic wrap, and so on. Label the tubes with the child's name, the artwork's date, and other descriptive information. Use sturdy liquor boxes with dividers to hold the cardboard tubes.

Rearrange the furniture in children's rooms periodically.

According to feng shui, changing your furniture arrangement can change your life—literally. Because children change very quickly, it's a good idea to reposition their furniture periodically so it doesn't stifle kids' growth. Rearranging the furniture also gives a room a fresh appearance. Who knows, in the process you might even find a few things you thought were lost forever!

CHAPTER 10

Paper Tigers: Home Offices

Clear your desktop.
Think of your desktop as prime real estate—only the most essential items deserve a place here. If you don't use it every day, it doesn't belong on your desktop. Move the rest to drawers, file cabinets, bookshelves, storage closets, and so on.

Don't just relocate paperwork, do something with it.

In her book *Taming the Paper Tiger*, Barbara Hemphill points out that "A cluttered desk indicates a pattern of postponed decisions." Each time you handle and look at a piece of paper but don't do something with it, you avoid making a decision and waste time because you'll have to confront the same decision-making process again later on. Whenever you pick up a piece of paperwork, act on it, file it, or toss it. Don't just put it back down on your desk or in your in-box.

Unclutter your office to clarify career goals.

The office also represents your career goals and your potential for success. Office clutter, however, can muddy these goals or cause obstacles that may block your success. Clear up clutter—especially old stuff you no longer need—to remove impediments and confusion in work-related areas.

Unclutter your office to increase prosperity.

It's not hard to see the connection between the office and prosperity. Both symbolically and practically, a well-organized office can lead to increased productivity. As discussed in Chapter 2, clutter in the office represents confusion about money matters. It can also signify obstacles that may be causing difficulties with clients, coworkers, and colleagues. By putting your office in order, you demonstrate a willingness to deal with problems involving your finances and to increase your income.

Keep an extra set of necessities in your workplace.

A co-worker of mine who was allergic to bees was once stung at work and had to be rushed to the hospital. If she'd had the foresight to keep her medication in her office drawer as well as at home, she might have been spared a great deal of trauma. Be prepared for lesser emergencies too. Keep a spare pair of glasses, contact lenses, and pantyhose, as well as extra tampons and medications, in your desk, locker, or work area, just in case.

Use one filing system only.
Develop a filing system that works for you—alphabetical, chrono-logical, by subject—and stick with it. Be consistent.

Put receipts in a shoe box.
If you can't commit to neatly organizing business-oriented receipts into expense categories as you generate them, make a few notations on them so that you'll remember what they pertain to, and then put them in a shoe box. When tax time rolls around, you'll at least have safely stored all those scraps of paper in one place, so your accountant can deal with them.

Get a spam-blocking program to stop unwanted email clutter.
Spam email clutters your computer and wastes your time. Treat it the same way you'd treat paper junk mail—trash it without opening it. Better yet, stop it before it starts with a spam-blocking program or directly through your access provider.

Reduce the number of places stuff can collect.

Keep the number of receptacles and potential clutter sites to a minimum. Use only one in-box, for example. Don't provide additional surfaces for stuff to sit once your desktop, computer workstation, and credenza are loaded up. Don't acquire more file cabinets—clean out those you already have.

Get newsletters from organizations you belong to by email, if possible, to cut down on paper clutter.

Many organizations will gladly email newsletters and announcements to you, instead of sending hard copy by mail. When possible, arrange emailings to reduce paper clutter and waste.

Clean out your in-box.

If paper has been sitting in your in-box for more than a month, its timeliness has probably expired. If you no longer need old paperwork, recycle it; otherwise, file it for future reference.

Cull your files regularly.

It's easy to stash paperwork in a file cabinet and forget about it for years. Schedule a date—every six months or so—to clean out your files. If you're certain you'll never need paperwork again, recycle or toss it. Store finished jobs that you might want to refer to again in clear plastic bins. Label the bins and put them in a storage room, attic, or other area instead of letting them take up precious space in your file cabinet.

Clear numbers from "caller ID."

If you have caller ID, every phone call that comes into your office or home gets recorded on your system. Although it may be convenient to store numbers for a day or so—especially those you plan to call back promptly—transfer phone numbers to a more permanent site as soon as possible, such as a Rolodex or address book. You won't have to shuffle through dozens of numbers to find the one you want and you won't risk losing a number if your phone message system goes down.

Clean out "cookies" regularly.

At least once per week, delete "cookies" from your computer. These electronic imprints are automatically stored each time you visit an online site. Not only do they take up room in your computer, they attract the attention of spammers who'll then jam your email with lots of unwanted junk.

Do you really need the latest and greatest computer equipment?

It may be tempting to update your computer every time a hot new model comes out, but most of us don't really need the latest and greatest equipment. My elderly neighbor, for example, just bought a state-of-the-art system that's far beyond his word-processing and email needs. In many places, old computer equipment can't be disposed of with your regular trash. It has to go to special waste sites (in my town, we have to pay to get rid of old electronic gear). Wait until you really need to update before investing in new equipment.

Organize and update at least one old file per day.

Break down the task of clearing clutter from your file cabinets and make the task more manageable. Each day, go through one old file folder and get rid of all paperwork that is no longer relevant or necessary. You may find that by eliminating "old business" you make room, psychologically, to attract new business.

Categorize files as "active" or "inactive."

As you get used to organizing and updating your files on a regular basis, you'll need to establish a place to move files you aren't using presently—you don't want to waste space in your primary work areas. The cartons printer paper comes in make good storage boxes for holding those files you aren't ready to part with completely. Label the boxes and store them in a closet, attic, or garage. Only current business should remain in your main file cabinets.

Arrange material in your files chronologically.

After you've removed all the old, outdated paperwork from your files, organize what's left in each folder in chronological order. Put the most recent materials in front and older papers in back. Now you can easily see the progression of a project and stay up-to-date on its developments.

Use rolling files in your office.

File storage units on wheels make it easy to roll current files around your office, so you can work with them at your desk, your computer, and so on. When files are no longer timely, move them from the rolling unit to a stationary file cabinet.

Use portable file boxes.

If you carry files between your office to home, or need to keep some in your car, portable plastic file boxes with handles can be convenient. These inexpensive containers can also be a handy way to organize materials on a project-by-project basis.

Leave some space in your file drawers.

Although it may be better in some ways to get paperwork off your desk and into your file drawers, just cramming those drawers full of stuff isn't the answer. From the perspective of feng shui, a jam-packed file drawer suggests you don't have room to take on any new business. Productivity expert David Allen recommends keeping your drawers no more than 75 percent full. When you start exceeding that limit, it's time to weed out old paperwork.

Sort paperwork into piles according to urgency.

If you don't have time to file paperwork right away, at least organize it into piles according to urgency: Sort things that need immediate attention in one pile, things that can wait a day or so in another pile. As soon as possible, file paperwork away in its proper place so you can find it when you need it and keep paper clutter at bay.

Transfer information from hard-copy files to your computer.
You can cut down paper clutter considerably and free up room in your file cabinets and your office by converting hard copy to electronic files. Scan documents and store them in your computer. Whenever possible, ask that correspondence be sent to you via email instead of on paper. If you keep your computer files well-organized, you'll find it's usually quicker and easier to access information from an electronic file than a physical one.

Use lateral file cabinets instead of vertical ones.
Lateral files provide more usable storage than vertical ones—and they're more convenient. Files don't get "lost" in the back of drawers, and because the drawers aren't as deep, they don't stick out so far into the room when open. You can use the top of a lateral file cabinet as an extra work surface, too.

Create a reference library in your office.

Establish your own reference section in your office, away from your primary work area. Place all your reference materials there—books, computer CDs and disks, file folders, address books, and so on.

File computer documents in folders.

Don't allow electronic documents to clutter up your computer's desktop. File them away in an organized fashion and label them, so you can locate and access them easily. After you've done this, you may find that your computer boots up faster, too.

Store or file stuff near the area where it will be used.

Unless you are intentionally trying to force yourself to get some exercise, organize office materials and supplies so they are stored in the area where they will be used. Keep extra printer cartridges in a drawer near your printer, for instance. Put stamps, envelopes, and packing tape where you handle the mail.

Download files onto CDs, zip disks, or auxiliary drives.
Files you rarely use don't need to be kept on your computer's hard drive. Instead, download them onto CDs, zip disks, or other storage options to free up space on your hard drive.

> **TIP: Remember to back up anything important, so if your computer fails or is stolen you'll at least have copies of your data saved elsewhere.**

Hang plastic magazine holder bins behind an office door.
Plastic magazine holders, like the ones you see in doctors' offices, are great for storing faxes, mail, and other paperwork temporarily. These handy racks usually feature four, six, or more large pockets so you can organize paperwork by subject, date, status, or client. If several people work together in the office, give each person his or her own pocket.

Put a silverware tray in a desk drawer.

Plastic, wicker, or wood trays designed to hold silverware are perfect for keeping office supplies neat and handy. Slip one in a desk drawer to hold pencils and pens, liquid paper, glue sticks, paper clips, Post-It notes, and other small-scale staples you use regularly.

Pin photos on a bulletin board.

Instead of letting framed photos occupy valuable space on your desk, display your favorite pictures on a bulletin board. They'll take up less room and you can see them just as easily. Or, group several photographs in a "gallery" frame and hang it up.

Control power-cord clutter.

Is your office a tangle of cords? Tame them once and for all. Unplug computer, fax, telephone, and all other cords and straighten them out. Tie as many as possible together with large plastic trash-bag fasteners or pipe cleaners, so they stay orderly.

Make duplicate sets of important documents and family information.

In case of emergency, make it easy on friends, family members, and co-workers by providing them with duplicate sets of important information. Include such things as medications, allergies, doctors' names and phone numbers, attorney's name and phone number, children's schools and schedules, names and phone numbers of all close friends and relatives, and so on. Give a copy to anyone who might be called upon to pitch in during an emergency or who might be assigned the responsibility of contacting other key individuals.

Write it down.

Don't try to keep everything in your head—write it down so you don't clutter up your mind. Make lots of lists and update them regularly. My favorite solution for daily to-do lists is a blackboard. I like to use different-colored chalks to prioritize tasks: red for urgent, blue for pending, and so on.

Use Post-it notes sparingly.

Instead of writing a zillion notes to yourself on tiny pieces of sticky paper and posting them everywhere, keep a log of the things you need to do in a spiral notebook or three-ring binder. Not only do those little notes look messy, they can get lost easily and there's no good way to file them for future reference, if necessary. Another plus: You can carry a notebook with you to meetings and on business trips.

Include outcomes on your to-do list.

A to-do list shouldn't just remind you of what you still haven't finished: It should be a step toward completing those things. As you compile your list, write down outcomes as well. By directing yourself toward a clearly defined goal, you reduce the psychological (and perhaps physical) clutter involved in getting there and improve your chances of success.

Don't wait until you're overwhelmed to make a list.
To-do lists should be starting points. Don't wait until you have so much to do that you can't remember everything. Making a list relieves stress and lets you move information from your brain to the next stage of the completion process. Once a task is on paper, you are more likely to finish it.

Organize filed paperwork into subcategories.
Even if you diligently file paperwork in hanging folders, after a while those folders can become crowded. Make it easier to find paperwork by creating subcategories within each hanging folder. Use manila folders to hold papers in each subcategory and label them—you can easily remove one folder temporarily while leaving the rest of the file in its place in the cabinet. If you wish, color-code subcategories by using colored folders or colored tabs.

Stash small office supplies in a fishing tackle box.
This storage solution is perfect for people whose cars sometimes double as second offices. The tiny compartments in a fishing tackle box are ideal for holding paper clips, Post-it notepads, pens and pencils, and other small office supplies so they stay orderly and handy.

Organize paperwork in clear plastic envelopes prior to a business trip.
When you are getting ready for a business trip, or even an upcoming meeting, stuff paperwork, brochures, tickets, business cards, maps, and other paraphernalia temporarily into a large, clear plastic envelope with a clasp. Each time you come across something you think you may need to take along, slip it into the envelope—the clear plastic allows you to see what's inside. Later, you can transfer this temporary storage packet or its contents to a briefcase or suitcase.

> **TIP: Use different-colored envelopes for different topics, appointments, clients, and so on.**

Organize stuff for the future in accordion files.

Paperwork you'll need at a future date will stay orderly and handy if you store it in an expanding accordion file. Label file pockets by day, week, or month depending on your schedule. Organize invitations to upcoming events, notices of birthdays you want to remember, doctor's appointments, and car-repair dates in the accordion file, as well as business meetings and trips, so you don't forget or miss an important date.

Store important personal documents where you can grab them quickly.

Organize crucial documents such as passports, birth certificates, marriage and divorce papers, medical records, and insurance information in a folder or three-ring binder. Store it in a convenient place, where you can grab it quickly in case of an emergency.

Don't save bank deposit slips and ATM receipts forever.
These receipts have a short shelf life—or should. As soon as you receive your monthly bank statement and check to make sure all deposits and withdrawals have been properly recorded, toss the paper slips. Their purpose has been fulfilled.

Label electrical cords.
Don't guess which electrical cord is which—label them with small, individual tags that identify what connects to what.

Vacuum your keyboard.
Dust collects in your keyboard and can interfere with optimum functioning. Vacuum your keyboard periodically to remove dust, dirt, crumbs, and so on.

> **TIP: Don't eat or drink near your keyboard.**

Keep back up CDs and zip disks in a safe deposit box.
Don't take a chance on losing important data if your office under-goes a tragedy, such as a flood or fire, or if your computer is stolen. Back up all your important data regularly and keep an extra set of CDs and zip disks in a safe place outside your home, such as a safe deposit box.

Write notes on the backs of business cards.
When someone hands you a business card, make a few notes on the back to remind you how, where, and when you met this person. If you connected at a conference, write the name of the event and the date on the card. If this person's company name doesn't clearly say what services or products it offers, record this information for future reference. If you have a friend or colleague in common, note that person's name. Write down any special services or other infor-mation you think may come in handy later (or that you might not remember).

Hang drafting tools on a pegboard.

Pegboards, like the ones the Shakers used, provide convenient places for draftspeople and artists to hang their equipment. T-squares, plastic templates, and other drafting implements that can be too large or awkward to store in drawers and cabinets stay neat and handy on pegs.

Hang an old-fashioned medicine cabinet in your office.

An antique wooden medicine cabinet makes an attractive and convenient place to store small office supplies, such as Liquid Paper, Post-it notes, glue sticks, and paper clips, rather than letting them take up precious space on your desktop or desk drawer. Close the door and you can hide all that clutter. Another plus: A mirrored cabinet lets you check your hair or makeup before meeting a client.

String a clothesline in your office.
Instead of an "in-box," string a clothesline in your office and hang time-sensitive papers on it with clothespins. This "in your face" method makes it harder to ignore paperwork or to pile other stuff on top of important papers.

Use an address book for websites.
An address book is perfect for keeping track of websites you like or visit regularly. Instead of listing sites alphabetically by name, group them according to products or services. For instance, designate tabs in your online address book for such things as housewares, clothing, specialty foods, electronics, office products, and so on.

CHAPTER 11

Hiding Places: Closets

Aim for versatile storage.

Rather than the conventional, single rod running the width of a closet, use a versatile—and adjustable—storage arrangement. Position clothes rods at varying heights to accommodate different-length garments. Shirts and pants, for instance, can be hung on rods placed above one another. Don't waste space at the bottom of your closet—build shelves and cubbyholes to hold shoes, handbags, and accessory items.

Get rid of clothes you haven't worn in a year.

In her book *Organizing Plain & Simple*, Donna Smallin gives this clutter-clearing axiom a positive spin: "Let's say…you have a whole wardrobe full of size eight clothing, but you've been a size twelve for the past five years. If you gave away all of your size eight clothing, and then did get back into the smaller size, the worst that could happen is that you would have to buy a new wardrobe. But wouldn't that be a great way to reward yourself for losing weight?"

Choose one "neutral" color, then build your wardrobe around it.

If you choose one basic "neutral"—black, navy, or brown—as the foundation color for your wardrobe and select only items that coordinate with it, you can reduce the number of garments in your closet. But, since everything goes with everything else, you'll actually get more use out of the clothing you own.

Get your colors done.

Most people look good in some colors, but not others. I highly recommend getting your "colors" done professionally. This technique helps you select clothing in the hues that flatter you and compliment your hair, eye, and skin color. Not only will you look better in what you wear, you'll be motivated to clear your closet of everything that doesn't suit you. Once you know what colors you can wear, you'll save time shopping, too, and you can bypass anything that's not in your color range. It's also a plus when it comes time to pack for a trip.

Shop with a trusted friend.

My friend Cally is ruthlessly honest and never hesitates to tell me when something I wear doesn't look good on me. If she vetoes a garment, I always let her "no" override my "yes." Cally's "just the facts, ma'am" approach makes her a wonderful person to take on a shopping expedition because she prevents me from buying clothes I probably won't (or shouldn't!) wear and saves me money.

Don't shop with friends if you are easily influenced.

It's easy to allow our friends' opinions to influence us. If you're the type who has trouble making up your own mind or who doesn't want to risk hurting a friend's feelings, you might be better off shopping alone. Remember, you're the one who has to pay for it and find a place in your closet to store it.

Build a shoe shelf in your closet.

Closet bottoms are often underutilized areas that can be tapped for storing shoes neatly. Install a shelf the length of your closet, high enough so you can slip shoe boxes under it for double-decker storage. Position shoes you wear often on top of the shelf where you can reach them easily, and put special occasion or off-season shoes further back.

Close closet doors.

To prevent private matters from becoming public, remember to keep closet doors closed.

Weed through your closets with a trusted friend.

Sometimes we can let our emotional attachments to certain outfits ("I wore that dress to my son's wedding," or "that jacket belonged to my father") keep us from getting rid of them, even though we no longer wear them. Here's where an objective, straightforward friend can be a valuable asset. Sort through your wardrobe together and dispassionately assess which garments should be eliminated.

Organize closets to resolve private personal issues.

Because closets are places where we "hide" stuff—or at least keep it out of the public eye—they symbolize private personal matters. Messy, jam-packed closets suggest you may have a number of hidden issues that are causing confusion in your life. When you clear out old stuff from your closets, you might find some of your troublesome psychological problems start to clear up, too. Neatly organizing closets shows you are willing to sort through hidden issues that may have been causing difficulties for quite a while.

Tape photos of your shoes on shoe boxes.

Instead of wasting time opening shoe boxes to see what's inside, label them. Better yet, take pictures of your shoes and fasten them to the outsides of the boxes.

Reuse linen pouches for sweaters.

Sheets often come packaged in plastic zippered pouches. Reuse these pouches to protect sweaters from moths when you store them away for the winter.

Keep barrettes neat.

To keep hair clasps and ornaments orderly and convenient, clip them on a scarf, ribbon, or tie and hang it in the closet. Now you can do away with a barrette container on your dresser. This easy-storage method enables you to see your entire collection at a glance, so you can find the one you want quickly. It also prevents barrettes and clips from getting caught on each other.

Keep pins neat.

The same trick works to keep pins neat and handy. Fasten your pins to a scarf or piece of fabric, then clip the scarf/fabric to a skirt hanger. This clever storage technique frees up space in your jewelry box and makes it easy to find the pin you want without having to rummage through your entire jewelry collection. You're less likely to stick yourself, too!

Cut down on bed linens.

How many sets of sheets do you really need? Two sets per bed is usually enough—one set on the bed and one in reserve. If you use flannel sheets in the winter, you might expand that number to four sets maximum. You can further reduce your supply of bed linens if all of the beds in your household are the same size, or if you wash and dry your sheets as soon as you strip the bed, then put the same sheets (now freshly laundered) back on the bed. You'll also save time folding them.

Don't store photographs or film in clothes closets.
According to the Eastman Kodak Company, carpet beetles and other egg-laying insects may eat or damage photographic negatives, color slides, and unprocessed film. Protect your precious photos—don't store them in closets or chests of drawers where you also store clothing, linens, or fabric.

Hang a full-length mirror inside a closet door.
You can do away with an over-the-dresser mirror in your bedroom if you mount a full-length one inside a closet door.

Don't set aside a guest closet.
Unless your home has oodles of closets, don't waste precious space on a guest closet. Use your entryway closet for everyday storage.

Clean out your pockets.

Before you put away a garment, check the pockets. Remove coins, tissues, and anything else you may have stashed there, and either throw it away or put it in its proper place.

Convert a closet to a home office.

If you don't think you have room for a home office, think again. Place a pair of two-drawer file cabinets in a closet and lay a piece of Formica countertop or wood across them to create a desk. Install a shelf above the desk to hold office supplies. Voilá, an instant office. When you close the door, it looks like an ordinary closet. Your work area is completely contained, neat and out of sight.

Hang tablecloths.

Instead of folding tablecloths, hang them in a closet on heavy, wooden hangers. They'll look nicer, with fewer fold marks and wrinkles, and won't take up so much room in a buffet drawer or cabinet.

Hang extra bed linens.

If your home doesn't have a linen closet, you can store extra sheets and pillowcases in your regular clothes closet. Fold and hang them on heavy suit hangers—they'll stay neat until you're ready to put them on the bed. Store linens in the closets of the rooms where they'll be used: This method is more convenient than placing all sheets and pillowcases in a centrally located linen closet.

Get rid of wire hangers.

Wire hangers make creases in your garments. Worse, they can rust and leave stains on clothing. Switch to wood, plastic, or padded fabric hangers to protect your good clothes and keep them looking their best.

Repair clothing promptly.

Don't return garments to the closet with missing buttons, ripped hems, or other damage. Repair clothing promptly to save time and annoyance later on.

Unclutter your purse.

Recently I called a colleague on her cell phone and heard this amusing message: "Sorry I can't answer your call. My cell phone's lost in the bottom of my purse." Clutter has a way of collecting and multiplying in your purse. If you don't change pocketbooks often, make a point of cleaning out all the accumulated stuff once a week, such as old receipts, tissues, pens that don't work, empty lipstick tubes, and so on. You'll lighten your load and may even find something you've been looking for.

Keep a basket in each closet for emergency pick ups.

Sometimes you just don't have time to clean up properly before a friend stops over. For these instances, keep a basket in each closet so you can quickly scoop up all the clutter and stash it in the closet temporarily. Notice the word *temporarily*. As soon as possible, go back and put away all the stuff in the baskets.

CHAPTER 12

Cobwebs and Cracked Skulls: Attics and Basements

Store photographs, paper items, books, audio and videocassettes properly.

These items don't belong in your attic or basement. In the summertime, an attic's heat can cause discoloration and deterioration. The dampness, mold, and mildew present in most basements can also cause permanent damage. Store them in a dry place at room temperature.

Group holiday stuff by season.

Store decorations and special holiday items so you can find them easily. Put everything that relates to a particular festivity in its own box (or boxes)—don't pack Christmas-tree ornaments with Easter baskets. Label each box clearly. Then store them chronologically. When July 4th rolls around, you won't waste time looking between the Halloween costumes and the turkey platter for the flags and sparklers.

Box things you aren't ready to part with yet.

Some things may fall in the "maybe" category: potentially useful in the future or too good to get rid of yet. If you aren't ready to part with some items yet, pack them in a special "for later" box and label the box. You might want to date the box, too, so you know how long those items have been stored. At a later time, you can re-evaluate them. Are they really that important?

Clear your attic to relieve mental strain.

Your home's attic, as mentioned in Chapter 2, symbolizes the mind and intellectual issues. If you tend to stash lots of stuff in your attic, you may be exacerbating mental stress, headaches, confusion, or other problems. When you clear out clutter in your attic, you may discover that you feel less pressured or that your mental clarity improves. Some people even experience relief from headaches, sinus conditions, and other head ailments.

Clear your basement to remove old psychological issues.

The basement symbolizes your foundations, roots (heritage), and sense of security. As I illustrated in Chapter 2, a cluttered basement can suggest a sense of insecurity or old problems stemming from childhood situations. By clearing out old stuff from your basement, you show you are willing to get rid of deep-rooted attitudes, behaviors, or old baggage that may have been causing difficulties for quite a while. A clean, neatly organized basement can help provide household members with a stronger sense of security and stability.

Store children's clothing by age.

If you are saving older children's outgrown clothing for younger siblings, pack garments away according to age—six months, one year, two years, and so on. Label boxes by size, season, and sex, so you can easily find the articles you want when the younger children are the right age to wear them.

Store kids' clothes in plastic garbage bags.

You don't need fancy storage units to pack away kids' off-season clothes. Put clothing in large, plastic garbage bags and fasten them with twist ties. Make sure to label the bags so you don't accidentally throw them out with the trash!

Don't store musical instruments in an attic or basement.

Musical instruments are sensitive to heat, cold, and moisture. Store them in a spot where both heat and humidity remain relatively constant, away from extremes.

Store kids' projects in plastic bins.

School projects, arts and crafts activities, scout projects, and others that you want to save are best stored in plastic bins—you can see what's inside and dampness can't damage the contents. If you are storing materials belonging to several different children in the family, color-code the containers so everyone can find their stuff easily. Arrange bins chronologically, so the most recent projects are most easily accessible.

Store paperwork in plastic bins.

The same strategy works for storing paperwork, too. Keep clear plastic bins in your office and sort paperwork into them. Color-code and label bins so you know what's inside, such as tax materials, equipment warranties, financial matters, old job files, and so on. When you've finished working on a particular project or at the end of the year, store the color-coded bins in the attic or basement, and arrange them by year—the most recent ones should be the most easily accessible. This system keeps file drawers and work surfaces from getting overloaded.

Label artwork before storing it.

Take photos of your artwork before you store it. Protect paintings, mirrors, and other artwork by wrapping them in acid-free paper. Then place each picture between two sheets of foam board and tape them together securely. On the outside of the package, affix photos that show what's inside.

Store artwork and mirrors standing up.

You reduce the chance of breakage and other damage if you store artwork and mirrors upright, rather than laying them flat. (Ideally, art on paper or canvas shouldn't be stored in damp places or where temperatures vary considerably. Make sure to package paintings carefully if you plan to leave them in an attic or basement.)

Use stackable plastic shelving units under attic eaves.
Maximize your attic's crawl space by placing inexpensive, stackable plastic shelving units under the eaves. Shelving seasonal items, extra dishes, paperwork, and other stuff you only use occasionally makes it easy to access them and expands your attic's storage capacity.

Label off-season clothing so it can be easily identified.
If you store off-season clothing in boxes in your attic or basement, label the containers so you can find articles easily. Pack similar items together—corduroys in one box, turtlenecks in another, swimsuits in another, and so on. If you prefer, take digital or Polaroid photos of what's in each box and tape the pictures on the outside of the container.

> **TIP: Plastic or heavy canvas zipper bags with cedar inserts will protect clothing during storage.**

Wrap and label paint cans.

It's a good idea to save some leftover paint after you've finished painting a room, in case you need to do touch-ups. Because paint can freeze, it's best to store it in a basement where temperatures don't get below 32 degrees, rather than in an unheated shed or garage. To keep paint cans from rusting, wrap them in plastic. Label cans with the paint number and/or name, the room where you used it, and the date the room was painted. After a year, throw the paint out—by now, sunlight, smoke, age, and other factors have altered the color on the walls, ceiling, or woodwork so what's in the can will no longer match. If you like the color, however, write down the brand name and mix numbers for the future.

CHAPTER 13

Everything but the Cars: Garages

Clear passageways through your garage.

Many garages are inadequately lit and may not allow a lot of space to walk around cars. To make matters worse, we often try to navigate our way through the garage with our arms full of groceries and other packages. Clutter in the garage can lead to accidents, so make sure to keep walkways clear.

Move items you plan to get rid of into the garage.

Box or bag items you intend to give to charity or take to the dump, then move them into the garage—you're one step closer to disposing of them. But remember, they're not gone until you've actually deposited them at their final destination!

Unclutter your garage to facilitate mobility.

As discussed in Chapter 2, the garage, your car's home, symbolizes mobility and freedom. A cluttered garage suggests you may not be as flexible or independent as you'd like to be. Remove that old stuff and you may soon expand your horizons and your opportunities to travel.

Keep items you use to clean your car together in a bucket.

Keep detergent, cleaning cloths, wax, and other products you use to wash your car together in a bucket. Hang the bucket on a peg or hook in the garage, so it's out of the way and everything is handy.

Keep an emergency box in your trunk.

Just in case you ever need them, keep emergency items such as a flashlight (with extra batteries in a plastic container), umbrella and plastic rain poncho, paper towels, duct tape, scissors, sneakers, blanket, Swiss army knife, and matches in a plastic bin in your trunk. In another box, keep things you might need for your car, including jumper cables, motor oil, brake fluid, antifreeze, and a "Help" sign.

Don't use your garage as an "offloading" zone.

Yes, I *did* tell you to move stuff out of the house and into the garage, with the intention of taking it to the thrift store, dump, or recycling center later. Too often, though, clutter ends up languishing in the garage. My friend Lee eventually had to park his car in the driveway because the clutter from his house overflowed and filled up the garage as well. Once a week, deal with castoff stuff that you've temporarily stashed in the garage and make sure it leaves the premises permanently.

Keep a plastic bag for trash in your car.
Don't let trash accumulate in your car. Keep a plastic trash bag handy—and use it. Instruct everyone in the family to immediately place empty food containers and soda cans in the plastic bag to protect upholstery and carpets.

Clean out your car weekly.
Cars can easily become repositories for fast-food wrappers, empty soda cans, magazines and newspapers, clothes, toys, sporting accoutrements, mail, and so on. At least once a week, clear the clutter from your car, so you have room for passengers!

Don't let clutter collect on the dashboard.
Keep the dashboard of your car and the area by the back window free of clutter. Not only is it unsightly, clutter can interfere with your visibility and pose a potential driving hazard. If you have to stop quickly, clutter could even cause an injury.

Stash a phone directory in your car.

The omnipresence of cell phones has made it difficult these days to find a pay phone, much less a phone book. Under the seat of your car, put phone books of areas you frequently travel to, so you'll have the phone numbers and addresses of services, shops, and people handy when you need them.

Place a trash can in your garage.

A trash can conveniently placed in your garage is a good reminder to clean out the junk from your car on a regular basis.

Wash the inside of your car.

Keep the inside of your car neat and clean. Whenever you wash the outside, vacuum and wipe out the inside, too. Studies show that washing the exterior and cleaning the interior of your car regularly helps to maintain its value.

Hang bicycles on vinyl-clad hooks.

Hooks mounted from the ceiling keep bikes out of the way. Hanging bicycles also helps retard air loss from their tires.

> **TIP: Hang helmets and other bike–related gear on the handlebars so everything you need when you go for a ride is in one place.**

Dispose of old car batteries properly.

Battery acid is caustic, so don't leave old car batteries lying around your garage. Many dumps won't accept batteries—call your local DPW to find out how and where to dispose of them properly.

Throw out half-empty cans of automotive products.

Don't bother saving half-empty cans of motor oil, brake fluid, and so on. Rather than risk a messy spill, get rid of all that leftover gunky stuff.

Hang tools and equipment.

Wall-mounted racks, pegboards, and hooks keep shovels, brooms, rakes, and other tools neatly organized in your garage. Hang as much equipment as possible. Lightweight articles, items with long handles, ropes and hoses are obvious hang-up candidates, but use your imagination: the more stuff you can get up onto the wall, the more room you'll have to park your car.

Organize equipment in a like-goes-with-like manner.

Organize your gear so similar items are placed in the same area. Keep all auto-repair tools and equipment in one spot; general maintenance materials such as motor oil and antifreeze in another. If your garage also houses stuff that's unrelated to your car, such as paint, ladders, or recycling bins, separate them from the automobile products and organize them according to use.

Don't store paint in the garage.

Unless your garage is heated or you live in a warm climate, don't store paint here during the winter months. Frozen paint is useless.

Store antifreeze safely.

Antifreeze is poisonous. Store it in a safe place where children and pets can't get at it. If you spill any on the floor, clean it up immediately.

> **TIP: Other automotive products may also be hazardous. Read the labels and store them carefully.**

Save plastic bags for dog-walk cleanups.
Plastic bags from English muffins, loaves of bread, and rolled-up newspapers are the right size to use as "gloves" for cleaning up after your dog. Save plastic grocery bags, too, and hang them near the door where they'll be handy when you take Rover for his daily walk.

Keep cat box litter handy for spills.
If you do accidentally incur an oily spill, use cat box filler to sop it up.

TIP: Once the bag has been opened, pour the rest of the litter into a plastic container with a lid to keep it from spilling.

CHAPTER 14

Handy Tips for Handymen: Toolsheds and Workshops

Store tools in a shoe caddy.
Here's another use for the handy, door-hung shoe caddy. The convenient pockets are perfect for storing small hand tools like screw-drivers, pliers, and paint brushes, especially if your shop or tool shed is short on space.

Store frequently used tools in a plastic bucket.

Large plastic buckets (such as the ones spackling compound comes in) are perfect for housing tools you use frequently and must transport from one place to another. Simply toss stuff you'll need for a certain job into the bucket, so everything stays together and is handy when you get to the job site. You can expand your bucket's capacity and efficiency by outfitting it with a pocketed canvas "apron" designed to wrap neatly around the outside.

Store tools and equipment in the areas where they will be used.

This sounds simple enough, but many handypeople don't set up their work areas with task zones in mind. Instead of housing all your tools and equipment in a central location, create storage sites in each work zone so the items you use when performing a specific job will always be close at hand. Saw blades should be stored near the table saw, for instance.

Keep similar items together.

Organize tools and supplies so that similar items are kept together, as well as items that may be used on the same type of project. For example, all electrical items—extension cords, plugs, outlets, switches, and fuses—should be put in one place. Put all plumbing supplies in another. Keep woodworking tools in another spot, paint supplies in another, and so on.

Install shelves between studs in your toolshed or workshop.

If your tool shed or workshop lacks finished walls, leaving the bare studs exposed, utilize this space for storage. Install narrow shelves between the studs to hold small hand tools and miscellaneous gadgets.

Keep small tools neat in a silverware tray.

Drill bits, screwdrivers, files, rasps, and other tools will stay neat and orderly if you sort them in a silverware tray. Fit one or more inexpensive plastic trays into your workbench drawer(s) to hold small implements and hand tools.

Store clean paintbrushes in coffee cans or jars.
Recycle coffee cans and quart-size glass jars as containers for paint-brushes. Organize them handle-down by size, shape, quality, or task. General-use brushes can go in one jar, special stippling or decorator brushes in another, expensive boar bristle brushes in their own jar, disposable synthetics in theirs.

Rent specialty tools instead of buying them.
If you think you'll only use a particular tool once or twice, don't bother buying it. Many specialized tools can be rented by the day, some even by the hour.

Clear the air.
Good ventilation is a must in work areas where paint, glue, solvents, and other products containing chemicals will be used. Sawdust can also cause respiratory problems. Clear "air clutter:" make sure your shop is well-ventilated.

Collect tools in plastic milk crates.

Plastic milk crates provide lightweight, portable storage for tools. Collect items you normally use together or will need for a particular task in individual milk crates. Everything stays together in one place and can easily be transported from shop to job site. Another plus: Milk crates can be stacked or hung up on the wall, out of the way.

Store tall, thin items between studs.

The space between studs is also ideal for stashing strips of molding, long-handled tools, lengths of copper pipes, plastic tubing, and so on.

Wrap paint brushes and rollers in plastic wrap.

You needn't wash or throw away paint rollers if you don't finish a job at the end of the day. If you plan to continue working with the same paint in the near future, simply wrap your paint brushes or rollers with plastic wrap. They'll stay wet and pliable until the next time you use them.

Use a spice rack for nails and screws.
Recycle a kitchen spice rack along with its glass jars and use them to hold nails, screws, nuts, bolts, and so on. A spice rack keeps these small items handy up on the wall, rather than letting them clutter up drawer space.

Buy expensive or rarely used tools collectively.
Consider purchasing expensive, specialty tools with friends or family members. If you only use an item once or twice a year, it may not pay to own it, unless you share the cost in a collective manner.

Fix it or toss it.
It's been said that the difference between men's clutter and women's clutter is men will build a $5,000 shed around theirs and call it "tools." Do you have broken tools or equipment lying around that you plan to fix "one of these days"? If so, either repair them or get rid of them. There's nothing more useless than a nonfunctioning tool!

Store tools in a "Roundabout Roller" cart.

These convenient units are comprised of several drawers stacked together in a lightweight aluminum frame on wheels. Hand tools, paintbrushes, screws and nails, measuring tapes, and other small items stay neatly organized and handy in the individual drawers. Plus, you can easily roll the unit around your workshop and keep what you need right at your fingertips.

Pegboards are workshop essentials.

The trusty pegboard is a versatile, inexpensive workshop staple. Install one or more in your shop or shed to keep tools and equipment visible, organized, and convenient.

> **TIP: Draw or spray-paint outlines around the tools, so you can see at a glance if one hasn't been returned to its proper place.**

Make use of chests with lots of drawers.

Old dressers and chests of drawers that aren't attractive enough for the bedroom get a new life in the workshop or toolshed. Often you can pick these up at the local dump or yard sales. Chests with a lot of various-sized drawers, such as old apothecary chests, are ideal. Try to find pieces that stand about thirty-two to thirty-six inches high so they can double as work surfaces.

Use a magnetic knife strip in your workshop.

Magnetic knife strips keep screwdrivers, pliers, and scissors handy in your shop. Hang one above your workbench so you don't have to waste drawer space storing these frequently used tools.

Recycle old kitchen cabinets.

If you or someone you know is renovating a kitchen, save the old cabinets for your workshop or gardening shed. Many of the convenient storage inserts found in kitchen cabinets are perfect for holding tools.

Guys, you're gonna love this one.

A clever tip I read about in *Cut the Clutter and Stow the Stuff* comes from Pete Gagnon. He recommends using a six-pack holder to carry small tools and gizmos back and forth from the workshop. The individual pockets keep gadgets organized, and besides, the carriers are free and readily available.

Dispose of oily rags carefully.

Don't leave rags soaked with oil, turpentine, paint, or other flammable materials lying around your shop—they can be a fire hazard. Don't bunch them up and throw them in the trash can either. Hang oily rags up and let them dry completely before disposing of them. (Check with your local dump or department of public works to see if your area requires these materials to be deposited in a special waste site.)

Hang lightweight items from a piece of pipe.

Caulk guns, paint rollers, and other lightweight tools can be hung from a piece of metal pipe. Have your local hardware store cut a pipe to the proper length, then attach it at a convenient height from your ceiling. If your workshop is in the basement, you may have lots of pipes already in place, ready and waiting for you to utilize them!

Hang a fire extinguisher in a convenient place.

Keep a fire extinguisher handy by mounting it on a pole or stud in your garage or workshop. Remember to check periodically to make sure it's still operational.

Store nuts and bolts in a fishing tackle box.

Tackle boxes are perfect for storing nuts, bolts, screws, nails, and other small stuff. Underneath the tray, you'll even have room for a few basic tools, such as a screwdriver and hammer. A tackle box is smaller and easier to carry around than a full-size toolbox, too.

Nail baby food jars to the beams.
My friend Michael has found a permanent and handy way to store nails, screws, nuts, and bolts. He nails the lids of baby food jars to the bottom of the beams in his workshop, then fills the glass jars with small stuff. Whenever he needs a nail, he simply unscrews the jar. He can see what's inside each jar and the contents don't clutter up his workbench or drawers.

Store sandpaper in hanging file folders.
Hanging file folders, like the ones you use in the office, are perfect for keeping sandpaper conveniently organized. Sort sandpaper by grit size and place pieces of the same size in a manila folder. Then slip all the manila folders in a hanging file folder. Store the file folder in a large drawer or simply hang it on two nails on a wall, door, workbench, or pegboard.

Be careful where you store sharp tools.

Many tools have sharp points or edges—don't store these in places higher than your head. Think safety first and position any sharp or potentially hazardous items where they can't fall on someone and cause injuries. And remember to keep these tools out of the reach of children, preferably in a locked cabinet or closet.

Store chemicals and solvents carefully.

The same holds true when it comes to storing turpentine, paint stripper, solvents, and other potentially hazardous chemical products. Don't place these items on shelves above your head, where they could accidentally spill on someone. Liquid products that could burn, poison, or otherwise cause an injury should be kept in a place kids and animals can't access, preferably in a locked cabinet or closet.

Keep hoses, ropes, and cords neat.

Coil up hoses, ropes, and electrical cords and fasten them so they stay neat and untangled. Rubber bands can be used to secure standard extension cords; heavy-duty electrical cords can be plugged together when not in use. Get cords and hoses off the floor so you don't trip on them.

Sell tools you rarely use.

Used tools are often the first things to be snatched up at yard sales. Many consignment shops will resell tools that are in good condition, too. If you have tools you rarely use, consider selling them.

Keep twine from tangling.

Only Martha could have come up with this tip. In her book *Good Things for Organizing*, Martha Stewart recommends attaching funnels to the wall or a pegboard and nestling balls of twine in them. Run the string down through the neck of the funnel, where it will stay tangle-free and handy.

CHAPTER 15

The Grass
Is Greener:
Yards and Gardens

Paint the handles of gardening tools bright colors.

How many times have you laid down a trowel and lost it in the grass? Here's a "bright" solution from my editor Elly Phillips: Paint the handles of your gardening tools hot pink, bright orange, lime green, or fluorescent colors, and you'll be able to locate them quickly in your yard.

Organize equipment according to season.

Arrange tools and other equipment you use during the summer—grass clippers, garden hoses, and potting soil, for instance—in one place. Organize winter stuff, such as snow shovels, ice scrapers, and rock salt, in another spot.

Use an old golf bag as a garden tool caddy.

An old golf bag is a perfect place to stash rakes, hoes, and other long-handled garden tools. Stuff small items, such as seed packets, in the ball pockets. If you also have a hand cart, you can mount the golf bag on it and roll all your tools around the yard, then back to the shed when you've finished with them.

Store seed packets in a clear plastic box.

Unused or partially used seed packets stay fresh and dry when stored in a clear plastic box. Organize packs chronologically, with the oldest ones in front.

Condition garden tools after each use.

Properly cared for, good-quality garden tools should last a lifetime. One way to keep them in shape is to clean and oil them after each use. Fill a five-gallon industrial plastic bucket with sand and old motor oil. When you've finished working in the garden, plunge your tools into the oily sand to clean mud and grit from the tool blades and prevent rusting.

Discard broken flower pots.

At the end of warm weather, when you bring in plants for the winter, check flower pots. Throw out any that are broken or cracked.

Use illusion to make a path look longer.

This landscaping "fool the eye" trick makes a pathway appear longer than it is (and thus less cluttered). Create a border along the path, using taller plants at the beginning and shorter ones near the back. The shorter plants increase the illusion of distance.

Let a ladder double as a plant stand.

A six-foot ladder can hold dozens of small plants. Rest flowerpots on each of the steps as well as on the paint tray holder.

Corral hand tools in a bucket.

Industrial buckets, like the ones joint compound comes in, are great for housing small garden tools. Plunk all your trowels, clippers, and other implements in the bucket and carry them with you as you work. These sturdy buckets come with lids and can double as stools, too.

Store gardening tools safely.

Some garden tools have sharp points or cutting edges that could cause injuries. Don't take a risk by placing these items on a shelf or cabinet above your head, where they might accidentally fall on someone. Find a secure place to store them, preferably where children won't have access them.

Make sure to return garden tools after using them.
It's easy to misplace a tool. To keep count of what's out and what's been returned, hang all your gardening tools on a wall or pegboard and draw their outlines to show where they should be stored. You can easily spot which ones are missing.

Recycle seedling trays.
Most nurseries and garden centers will take back plastic seedling trays and pots if they're in good shape. Instead of throwing them away, recycle them.

Hang up lightweight plants in a greenhouse.
In a small greenhouse, orchids, bromeliads, and many other small, lightweight plants can be hung from the top of a greenhouse. One of my editors, Delilah Smittle, came up with this attractive way to expand the space in a small greenhouse: Affix a rack from the ceiling, then attach delicate plants to the rack.

Pour aquarium water on your garden.

When you change the water in your aquarium, don't just dump it down the drain. Pour nutrient-rich aquarium water on your plants to fertilize them.

Make your own rooting solution.

If you have a willow tree in your yard, cut up a branch and soak the pieces in water for a week. Remove the wood pieces, but save the water. To stimulate root production of new plants, soak the rooting ends in the willow water.

Compost leaves and grass clippings.

Instead of bagging leaves and grass clippings, compost them. Leaves and grass are nature's fertilizer—put them in the compost pile along with your kitchen scraps. Dried leaves can also be used to mulch and protect your plants during the winter.

Leave grass clippings in your yard.

If you use a mulching mower, you won't have to rake up grass clippings from your yard. Leave clippings to fertilize your lawn, instead of applying chemicals.

> **TIP: If you adjust the mower blade to leave grass a bit high, especially during peak summer heat, you won't have to water your lawn as often.**

Compost kitchen scraps.

You don't have to buy fertilizer—compost your kitchen scraps to feed your garden. Keep a plastic container or bucket with a lid under the sink and put vegetable trimmings, coffee grounds, eggshells, and fruit peels in it—no meat or greasy stuff, though. Empty the container regularly into an outside compost pile and turn the pile occasionally with a rake or garden fork. After about a year, your compost will have broken down enough to use on your garden beds. This practice reduces landfill waste and saves money as well.

Keep your lawn art gallery looking fresh.

When it comes to lawn ornaments, one person's kitsch is another's classic. Instead of letting your yard succumb to clutter, display your treasures the way art museums do—rotate them. Rather than filling your entire yard with statuary, bird baths, wrought iron *objets d'art*, and so on, choose a few pieces and let them serve as decorative accents. Periodically, update your display and put out different items.

Use illusion to increase the appearance of depth in a flower garden.

A spacious garden looks less cluttered. Bright, warm colors, such as red and orange, seem closer to us than they really are, while cool colors, such as blue, purple, and silver, seem to recede. To create an illusion of distance and make your flower beds appear larger, plant flowers in hot colors near the front and cooler colors in back.

> **TIP: In the gardening world, white isn't a "cool" color. Use white flowers as highlights.**

Reduce color clutter in your garden.

Instead of trying to include every flower species you like in your garden, limit yourself to several categories. Choose colors, shapes, and heights that compliment each other. Establish a color palette based on two or three main colors, and select plants in those hues only. Pay attention to the periods when various flowers bloom, and plan your garden so you'll have color throughout the growing season.

Add newspaper to your compost.

Shred or cut up old newspapers and add them to your compost bin to eliminate odors from decomposing grass clippings and the like. A little newspaper works like a charm in that kitchen compost bucket, too. And—Shredded paper also helps to reduce odor in your garbage can.

Group like with like.

For a sense of clutter-free harmony, create flower groups, rather than scattering plants randomly throughout the beds. For instance, plant clusters of impatiens or keep all the yellow tulips together.

> **TIP: Uneven numbers of plants in clusters will produce a more pleasing arrangement.**

Plan ahead.

The key to a great garden is planning. Sketch your beds on graph paper before you start—you'll save time, energy, and money. And you can avoid a cluttered look right from the start!

> **TIP: Expect to relocate plants periodically. A professional gardener I know says it may take three moves until you get everything just where you want it.**

Keep fertilizer and potting soil from spilling.
To keep open bags of fertilizer, lime, and potting soil from tipping over and making a mess in your garden shed, set them upright in large terra-cotta flower pots. Plastic storage bins, milk crates, and large buckets (like the ones that joint compound comes in) work well, too.

Screen gutters.
To prevent debris from building up in your gutters, cover them with screening or wire mesh.

Use gutter clutter as fertilizer.
If your gutters are already full of clutter, use that nutrient-rich debris to fertilize your garden.

Grow a garden for birds.

Make your garden do double duty! Birdwatchers can attract their favorite species by growing plants that birds love to eat. Plant sunflowers, purple coneflowers, black-eyed Susans, columbine, bee balm, salvia, and ornamental sages. If you have room, plant grains such as ornamental corn, millet, wheat, and sorghum, too. Scarlet runner beans will bring hummingbirds flocking to your yard. The birds will thank you!

Attract butterflies to your garden.

You can do the same thing for your butterfly friends. Butterflies prefer flat blossoms that they can use as mini landing pads. Daisies, Queen Anne's lace, cosmos, yarrow, and of course, butterfly weed are among their favorites. Monarch butterflies like ornamental milkweed, too.

Provide plenty of water for birds and butterflies.

If you want to attract birds, water is even more important than food. Provide a ready source of water for your winged friends. If you have a birdbath, place a few large stones in it so birds have a place to perch while drinking. Butterflies love water and mud. Make a mud puddle in your yard and watch the butterflies flock to it.

Get rid of aphids, safely.

Skip those messy pesticides. You don't have to use toxic chemicals on plants to banish aphids. Spray plants with a strong blast of water, making sure to douse the stems and undersides of leaves as well.

CHAPTER 16

Traveling Light: Travel Tips to Lighten Your Load

Carry essentials on the plane with you.
Don't check the things you'll need as soon as you arrive at your destination. Put them in a carry-on bag and keep them with you. If your luggage gets lost, at least you'll have necessities such as contact lenses, medications, and cosmetics handy.

Pack with Zip-Loc bags.

Plastic Zip-Loc bags come in handy when packing for a trip. Prevent messy spills by putting shampoo, cosmetics, and other liquid items in their own plastic bags. Put shoes in bags to keep them from soiling your clothes. Fold garments and slip them into larger bags to help reduce wrinkling. Pack articles that will be worn or used together in a single bag. Include an empty bag for dirty clothes.

Stuff your shoes to save room.

Socks, undies, jewelry, ties, belts, and other small items can be packed inside your shoes to save room in a suitcase.

Share with a friend.

If you are traveling with a friend or family member, share as many items as possible to minimize suitcase clutter. Take along only one hair dryer, shampoo, conditioner, toothpaste, and so on.

Pare down the amount of clothing you pack for a trip.
Most people take along far more than they need on trips. Choose clothing so that everything is in a similar color range—that way, each article coordinates with several others. If you're traveling during cold weather, think in terms of layers so you don't have to pack a lot of bulky garments. Because shoes can be heavy and take up a lot of room in your suitcase, wear the clunkiest ones while you're traveling and pack the lighter ones.

Reduce wrinkles.
Place sheets of tissue paper between your clothing when you pack to help reduce wrinkles.

Reuse plastic food containers for jewelry.

Clear plastic containers from the supermarket can be reused to hold jewelry when you travel. If necessary, use several small containers and keep all pieces of one color or type in each container. Plastic vitamin containers are great, too, for holding earrings, rings, pins, and small items.

Keep a list of credit-card numbers.

Make a list of all your credit-card numbers and the 800 numbers for reporting them, in case your credit cards are lost or stolen when you are traveling. Give a trusted friend or relative the list to keep for you, so the information is readily available if you need it.

Recommended Reading

Alexander, Skye. *10-Minute Clutter Control*. Gloucester, Massachusetts: Fair Winds Press, 2004.

Alexander, Skye. *10-Minute Feng Shui*. Gloucester, Massachusetts: Fair Winds Press, 2002.

Aslett, Don. *Clutter's Last Stand*. Cincinnati, Ohio: Writers Digest Books, 1984.

Baird, Lori, ed. *Cut the Clutter and Stow the Stuff*. Rodale Inc., 2002.

Hackett, Kathleen, ed. *Good Things for Organizing*. New York: Martha Stewart Living Omnimedia, Inc., 2001.

Hemphill, Barbara. *Taming the Paper Tiger*. Washington, D.C.: Kiplinger, 1997.

Kingston, Karen. *Clear Your Clutter with Feng Shui*. New York: Broadway Books, 1999.

Smallin, Donna. *Organizing Plain & Simple*. North Adams, Massachusetts: Storey Publishing, 2002.

Skolnik, Lisa. *The Right Storage: Organizing Essentials for the Home*. Gloucester, Massachusetts: Rockport Publishers, 2001.

About the Author

Skye Alexander is the author of 10-Minute Feng Shui and, 10-Minute Clutter Control, as well as 10-Minute Magic Spells, 10-Minute Tarot, 10-Minute Crystal Ball, The Care and Feeding of Your Chi, Magickal Astrology, and Planets in Signs. Her first mystery novel, Hidden Agenda, won the Kiss of Death Award for the year's best book of romantic suspense. Her stories have appeared in several anthologies, including Undertow and Riptide, and have been translated into German, Portuguese, and Korean. In 2001, she was filmed for a Discovery Channel special performing a magic ritual at Stonehenge. She lives in Massachusetts with her feline assistant, Domino.